Your
Psychic
Power

also published by Piatkus

The Psychic Explorer
by Jonathan Cainer and Carl Rider

Your Psychic Power

and how to develop it

A STEP-BY-STEP GUIDE

Carl Rider

PIATKUS

To Meredith and Hannah

© 1988 Carl Rider

First published in 1988 by
Judy Piatkus (Publishers) Ltd of
5 Windmill Street, London W1

Reprinted 1994, 1996

British Library Cataloguing in Publication Data

Rider, Carl
    Your psychic power: a practical guide to developing
    your natural clairvoyant abilities
    1 Clairvoyance
    I. Title
    133.8′4

ISBN 0-86188-775-1
      0-86188-880-4 (Pbk)

Designed and illustrated by Zena Flax
Items for the cover supplied by Mysteries, Covent Garden, London

Phototypeset in 11/12 pt Compugraphic Goudy Old Style
by Action Typesetting Ltd, Gloucester
Printed and bound in Great Britain by
Biddles Ltd, Guildford and King's Lynn

CONTENTS

INTRODUCTION

Everyone has had a psychic experience, at some time, no matter how insignificant. Think about it, and you will find it is true. For example, a letter may have been anticipated, a feeling of foreboding turns out to be correct, you experience an inexplicable attraction, and so on.

We are *all* born psychic, it is simply a forgotten art that needs to be relearned.

Many people have the vague feeling that if they could just organize their intuitive near-misses, they would be genuinely psychic. This book will help them to do just that. If you, too, find yourself fascinated by all things psychic, but do not regard yourself as being particularly gifted, this book will give you your chance to take a practical step toward converting your enthusiasm for psychic things into actual psychic experience. Discover and try out for yourself techniques such as clairvoyance, psychometry (reading objects), crystal ball gazing, tea-leaf reading, prophecy, clairaudience, astral projection, aura perception, etc. (note: not spirit mediumship). Practical guidance is given in all these traditional techniques.

This book goes one step further. It is not simply a how-to-do-it manual. As every practising psychic knows, instructions are not enough in the extremely personal world of supersensible perception. What is vital, is to teach the correct attitude. Success with all these exciting psychic techniques comes automatically and easily, if they are approached in a certain frame of mind. This frame of mind requires you to look at yourself, to begin to notice the way you think, and what kind of person you are! Don't worry! You will be pleasantly surprised.

Since ancient times, clairvoyance has developed as a side effect of raising your personal awareness to the highest possible level. To become a 'sensitive' you must first be sensitive to your own inner ways and foibles. Then suddenly, easily and automatically your psychic power will be realized. That's the way it has always happened. That's how effortlessly it will happen to you.

What then is this required frame of mind, this attitude that can bring you everyday use of your natural psychic power? Read on. What follows are practical exercises and safe guidance on every aspect of this power, and how to experience it. You will be taken stage by stage through all those vague intuitions and quiet feelings that, when put together, make up the psychic frame of mind.

1
THE STARTING POINT: PSYCHIC SQUARE ONE

I hope you will already feel fairly certain of the fact that everyone has a natural psychic sense. It is important that you do not start off with the feeling that you are trying to do the impossible, or that others are actually better qualified than you to have clairvoyant experiences. Obviously, you may not be able to shake off these reservations completely, simply as a result of reading the last few paragraphs, but you must at least have the feeling that you can expect to have some psychic experience after doing the exercises in this book.

In this chapter we will begin to lay the basis of sound psychic sense, but first let me give you a 'golden rule' that you are going to hear a lot more of as we go along: your psychic experience must always be under your control.

This book may be read by people with widely differing psychic backgrounds, so I must start on a rather serious note. Many people think that psychism is 'dangerous', or harmful. It is not. For most of us it will be a comfortable step in a new direction. But there is a part of every 'psychically inclined' person, that does need a good talking to. So, lets get it over with!

It really doesn't matter if, to date, you have had the most spectacular clairvoyant visions. However dramatic those psychic experiences may have been, from now on you must strive for consistency, a psychic state that you can control. If your clairvoyance has been the kind that breaks through when you least expect it, leaving you looking for interpretations and explanations, then try to lay those memories to one side. Or, if you are already prone to profound psychic revelations, and regard yourself as a 'natural psychic', try to forget your experiences so far. From now on go for stability and modesty. I have a good reason for stressing this.

Sudden 'natural' clairvoyance often brings with it scope for wild attacks of egoism – and the possibility of all sorts of errors. So often, sudden psychic breakthroughs can lead to confusion and upsets, and that I do not want to encourage. So please don't become like so many people I have met. Lovely people, who have seen many things, from angels to a long-lost Hungarian grandfather. They have heard the Music of the Spheres, and even performed the miraculous, but they are sad and distraught with wondering about their powers. Their minds are plagued with thoughts such as: 'Where did my special power come from?' 'What must I do?' 'Why me?' 'Am I somehow chosen?' 'What does this mean?' Or, 'Oh dear, I must have done something terrible; this is weird!' They often resort to telling people about their experiences in the hope of gaining a little better understanding of themselves. Inevitably they then lapse into embroidering and enlarging on their stories. After all, it is hard to resist the urge to entrance people with accounts of unearthly achievements, especially if everyday existence is a bit mundane. Even more ironic, is the fact that exaggeration, delusion and self-deception are actually normal and forgivable parts of clairvoyant experience, to be studied and worked with. (It is a fact that clairvoyant experiences don't store properly in the ordinary human memory. They naturally distort there.) Our unhappy 'natural' psychics do not know this however, and often become the victims of guilt, adding unjustified feelings of dishonesty to their burden.

So please watch out, there is a great possibility of wasting your psychic potential in this way. Be deliberately modest about your experiences, or you might find yourself having just one psychic experience every ten years, because you spend the rest of your time talking about it!

Be very clear in your mind that you are aiming for a steady and controlled psychic growth. That is what this book is designed to bring you. Let your sixth sense bring you spontaneous, small but consistent results over a long period. If what you really hanker after is sensational dialogues with long-gone historical characters (and many do!), or if you want a glimpse of the Archangel Gabriel, or a vision of tomorrow's racing pages, then somewhere along the line you have picked up the wrong idea about psychic experience. Try to put it down.

Psychics *do* see visions, and clairvoyants *can* speak with authority on behalf of long-dead people, but certainly none who can will be shouting about it. However, *all* who can will tell you that it is important to keep your psychic powers strictly under control. So let the professionals and any so-called experts get on with their clairvoyant investigations in their own way. They probably never had the early benefit of a sympathetic guide such as this. Most experienced psychics had to do a lot of private experimenting and suffering to bring their powers into line with the requirements of a relatively normal daily life.

So (one more golden rule), please don't try to run before you can walk. Believe me, a psychic walk will be quite exciting enough! Let the fact that you have picked up this book be clear evidence of your curiosity and willingness to learn. Hang on to those two qualities tightly, and use them to make steady and reliable progress into your own abilities, with the guidance of the chapters that follow.

If you feel you are just on the brink of developing dramatic superpowers, try to be patient. Otherwise, you may soon find that your expectations block you from seeing the delightful possibilities that lie all around you, waiting to be taken up simply and effortlessly.

Now for some encouragement! Most of us do not realize what powers we have. From my own observations, it is by no means always the flamboyant extrovert with the immediate charisma who possesses the talent. Many 'ordinary' people who would not dream of calling themselves clairvoyants have far greater reserves of insight. They are unaware of it, yet they draw on it daily in an unconscious way. If such a person makes a sincere effort to stimulate his/her already well-formed powers in even the tiniest organized way they can easily release enough psychic energy in themselves to encompass all the spectacular and high flown claims of many a professional 'psychic'.

Developing your intuition

Let's start to learn. Psychics, as people, are often emotional and unpredictable. This has given rise to a popular idea about psychic ability that is totally wrong. I must put it right. The popular view goes like this: 'Psychism is a wildly intuitive and erratic process. It cannot be taught, but comes in vague bursts. Even if it could be taught, the teaching of it would probably be wild, vague and illogical.' I must tell you that this is not true. Intuition can be developed and taught, logically. In fact, the seeds of psychic awareness are always sown in the world of logic. The best way to start up the intuitive processes is through the use of your cool, calculating intellect, because thoughts are the starting point for intuition. I know it sounds hard to believe at first. A novice might expect to have to do some very airy and nebulous exercises to induce the correct 'intuitive' frame of mind. But no. Thought is the best, and totally guaranteed way of making a sound and safe start towards clairvoyant awareness.

I hope that this comes as good news. Thoughts are the one thing that most of us have in abundance. We are all pretty well earthbound and to some extent 'boring' when it comes to tales of glory of a psychic kind. But simple thinking is something we all do. So let me tell you one more time: psychic awareness begins with your thoughts.

The natural psychics and the miracle seekers among you may feel a little let down by this apparently down-to-earth, unspiritual approach to the psychic realms, but it is true nevertheless. Try it and you will see. The best way to start up a sleepy and little used intuitive ability is to prod it with thoughts. And that is exactly what we are going to do in this chapter. I guarantee that, pretty soon, it will wake up, slowly stretch itself and get busy for you.

There is a huge emotional side to it all too, but we'll come to that later. Never fear that this is going to become an 'eggheads only' situation, however. You are not going to be presented with abstract equations and IQ tests to think about. What you will turn your cool clear commonsense to is much more interesting, the most fascinating of all subjects — without a doubt everyone's favourite. You must think about YOU.

A word about expectations. We are all eager to learn about psychic matters and the growth of our intuitive abilities, and this is a very good thing. I expect by now, in the back of our minds, we all have a pretty clear idea of the sort of things we want to know, and in what direction we want to go. However, there is a slight catch. In psychic matters more than any other subject in the world, 'having a pretty clear idea of what we want to know and where we want to go', far from being a good starting point, is actually a positive disadvantage! The psychic learning process, though logical, is different from all others. For psychic purposes you must forget where you want to go, and start by learning about where you are. Only then will you make progress.

Crossing the line

In order to use your psychic senses, you need to cross a very special line. Let me tell you about this line. On this side of the line is the ordinary world you know about. On the other side is a different land. The ways and means of learning and finding things out that you have worked to perfect since childhood have all been developed on this side of the line. Over there, they simply won't reveal anything. So be aware of the possibility that everything that you know and are sure of to date is completely irrelevant.

To all intents and purposes we are psychically blind; our organs of psychic sense are not developed yet (although we all possess such organs. We can't simply step over to the other side. So the best way to start learning about what is on the other side is to look clearly at what is going on on this side. Then, as and when we are carried spontaneously and gently over, we will have more chance of actually seeing what is there. We will not swamp the first subtle glimmers of our new sense, by cramming it into the old patterns. We will be so well aware of the feel of the experiences we already know that the new psychic feelings will stand out clearly against them.

So the first exercises are deliberately down to earth! They are about you, your personality and your life.

But first, back to this special dividing line. Try to follow closely, part of the first exercise — using your logic to set your clairvoyant abilities in motion. This side of the line, the non-psychic side in which we are completely at home, is the world of senses. In this world we rely entirely on our senses for finding things out. Eyes, ears, nose, mouth, skin, all give us news about what is going on around us. Everything that has happened in your life came in through these gateways of the senses. Stop where you are right now and look around; feel your skin, listen, and sniff the air. Life's experience is all around you, and flooding in through your senses.

Actually you could be forgiven for never realizing that you have such things as senses at all. You could quite naturally think that there was just life and living: things to do and things to look at . . . and eating . . . and talking . . . and going to places . . . and all the other myriad things that go to make up the day. As a philosopher might say: to know what something is , you have to have something else to compare it to.

Then, one special day in your life arrives. You suddenly see something that nobody else sees, or hear something that no one else hears, or simply 'know' something out of the blue, all of a sudden. What do you do then? You cannot deny that you have seen, heard or known something, yet it must have arrived in your mind through some other route, otherwise everyone else would be aware of it too. You can either shrug the whole thing off, or you can conclude that there is some other way of getting through to your mind that doesn't involve seeing, hearing, eating, doing, and all the other activities you knew before. You will then become aware of your senses, simply

because for the first time in your life you will have learned something *without* using them.

Only when you become deeply aware that you have senses can you start getting information *without* using them.

Non-sensory understanding (extra sensory perception, ESP it used to be called) is actually a very normal thing, but as you will now begin to see, it does have its tricky and elusive side. Perhaps the main thing that makes it so difficult to grasp is that ESP gives you such a surprising feeling when it actually happens to you. One tiny experience produces a flood of questions and reactions. So much so, that you probably won't get a sniff of it again for a long time afterwards! The mental turmoil caused by the simple arrival in your mind of a message that didn't come through your senses is usually out of all proportion to the information you actually received. For example suppose that you dream that Aunt Hilda will pay a surprise visit next Tuesday, and then she does . . . well, then that one tiny scrap of information suddenly becomes the centre of excitement and amazement! But, as in all things, a little understanding helps. Let's go back to the idea of the line that divides the two worlds.

This side of the line is the world dominated by our senses. So what is on the other side? Well, the simple answer is: thoughts. Thoughts

... those things which I mentioned earlier as the best way of prodding the psychic powers into action. The other side of the line is the world of thoughts. And knowing this, it is quite easy to start the journey from one side to the other. We all do a great deal of thinking. Apart from breathing, it's probably the one thing we all do most of, so we should all be able to make it across fairly easily.

Look at it like this. Thoughts come from outside, from the world of your senses. And where do they go? They go inwards, past and behind your senses, into you. Your mind converts the world around you, as revealed by senses, into thoughts. So thoughts can carry you to the other side of the line, beyond your senses so to speak. We are pretty well one hundred per cent dominated by these senses, and they don't loosen their iron grip that easily! Even when you are in bed under the covers in the pitch dark, totally silent, having a quiet think, you are still at the mercy of the sense world. You are only able to think about things that are visible to, and brought to you courtesy of the senses. They will still be there, dragging you out to the sense side of the line again.

However, consider this. It will help to strengthen your feeling for the inner, psychic side of the line. Though your thoughts may be about the world around you, they have one major asset that makes them very significant in this business of psychic learning. They move about vigorously inside your head! You can feel them in there. You can also listen to them. They may be all about what is outside of you, but they take place inside of you. You can hear something active in there, and where your thoughts are moving, is the beginning of where the psychic you actually lives.

So psychic awareness starts off with activity in your head. You will benefit greatly in your first attempts at psychic growth if you develop a feel for this idea of yourself as a being inside your own head, witnessing information as it flows in. Once again, let me stress this is only the first of many stages. Don't seize upon it and stay with it from now on, or you will limit your growth. The idea to cultivate is that once you were outside, but now you are inside. That is what crossing this dividing line is all about.

Getting there

That is enough on the abstract side for now. Let's get down to some exercises involving you in less reading, and more doing. I realize that doing exercises written in a book is a lot different from doing them under the watchful eye of a live teacher, who can actually tell you step by step what to do, as he or she sees you getting the hang of it. But be reassured; these exercises have been specially designed to work on their own.

The best way of approaching this section is to read all the exercises through, stopping every now and again to do the exercises, or parts of exercices that make you feel you want to put the book down and try them straight away. Later, you can have another look to see if you can pick up some more of the chosen exercise. After a while, in some cases you will be able to do the whole exercise, and re-do it at your leisure.

Whatever you do, don't work through systematically, making sure you have got everything exactly 'right'.

Some exercises involve the use of pencil and paper but, even with these, feel free simply to read through at first giving them a little casual thought. Come back later, and get more into them. Then start writing things down. The act of writing things down has an almost magical effect on the way your minds works.

One more thing. The act of organizing yourself: getting a pen and paper, and putting time aside for intuitive development, is actually a powerful exercise in itself, particularly in the early stages of clairvoyant growth. As I said earlier, many of us already have a huge reservoir of well organized psychic energy at our disposal. The act of deliberately sitting down to do a psychic exercise might be just the trigger we need to produce results apparently out of all proportion to the scope of the exercise. It is important that, after completing an exercise, you take the time to 'ground' yourself, or return to normality from your heightened plane of awareness. This can be achieved by a simple act, like making a cup of tea, fixing yourself a snack, or even going to the toilet.

EXERCISE: Pie chart

This exercise will help you to look at yourself, and to find the space for your psychic growth.

1 First, draw a circle, to represent your time in the waking day.

2 Draw 'slices' in the circle as if dividing up a cake or a pie. Draw the slices bigger or smaller according to the proportion of time you give to the different activities those individual slices represent in your average day: i.e. time given to work; time given to the children; time given to travel; time given to the house and domestic things; time given to others and, most importantly, time

given to yourself alone. Draw up the pie chart with as much
honesty as your can muster.

When you actually see your 'life' laid out in black and white in front
of you like this you will be greatly surprised. The fact is that most of
us give practically no time at all solely to ourselves. We are constantly involved with other people and other purposes.

Now let's take a closer look at the second reason for doing this
chart. Your psychic growth has got to be fitted into the tiny 'you and
you alone' section.

Although you may have a very busy and fulfilling time in all the
other departments of your daily life, when it comes to your psychic
development, you are most definitely on your own. Psychic growth
is a totally individual and private matter, between you and you
alone. So you had best be prepared for this. Many people do not like
the idea of being alone and may be put off by this thought, but I'm
afraid there is no way round it! What I can say however is that if
there is the slightest chance that you *can* bring yourself to accept
this idea, try, and you will open up a huge new area of potential in
yourself. It is essential to understand that what you learn psychically
speaking is for yourself, and yourself alone. Don't worry though, you
are not going to become sullen and introverted all of a sudden. Your
pie chart will confirm that. Take another look at it. It will show you
clearly that all your other activities and friends will still make up by
far the largest proportion of your life.

You need time for yourself because you are going to discover your
psychic abilities, deep within yourself. If you continually spend all
your time thinking only about what is going on around you, you will
never get in touch with them. Similarly, if when you do get in touch
with them, you instantly try to project them outside you into the
sense world, say, by constantly talking about them, or trying to help
your children by using them, then you will wear them out before
they have time to grow strong.

EXERCISE: *Thought pie*

Here is another exercise to set you looking at yourself.

1 *Draw the pie circle again.*

2 *This time, make each slice represent the amount of thinking time*
   you give to different subjects.

Possible topics include: thoughts of money, plans and ambition, love and sex, going over old arguments, jealousy, dreaming of things you want etc. The list could be quite long if you really get down to it, but don't let that put you off. Try to get in front of you a general pattern of the things that go through your mind daily. It's a tricky thing to get your mind round, but stay with it. It's easier to make a list first, and then do the chart. Don't leave your chart lying around though; it could be embarrassing.

I think you will notice two things from doing this exercise: how many and varied are the subjects that race through your mind and how thoughts are actually all the same — i.e. they are all traceable back in one way or another to our senses.

My reason for pointing this out again is that later on you will be deliberately trying to use your mind to think thoughts that are not based in the senses. Believe me, there are such thoughts. When you actually come to do it, you will find it has quite a powerful and pleasant effect. You see, one of the purposes of this exercise is to suggest to you the possibility that, to date in your life, a large part of your absence of psychic ability is simply a result of not giving any mental room to even a single psychic or spiritual idea. People have little or no clairvoyant experience, because they have little or no clairvoyant thoughts in their heads!

Many people find this suggestion a bit too simple to be credible. I can assure you however, especially at the earlier stages, nothing could be truer. In psychic matters of all kinds, tiny things often have effects that are miles out of proportion to what you would expect. It takes little more than the addition of one or two genuinely non-sense based thoughts, slipped in among all those millions of others, to produce the most amazing changes in the way you perceive.

You will be trying it later on, so you will see. For now, however, stick to these deliberately sense-based development exercises.

EXERCISE: *Friends like these*

1 *Make a list of all the people you know. Write down their names in any order. Spend time searching your memory to remember people from the past.*

2 *Now put their names in order of preference!*

I realize that in any sensitive way, this second step is not possible and certainly not fair, because different people will mean different things to you. Nonetheless, this is no excuse. In this exercise be ruthless! Work toward a definite and clear cut list. By the way, make sure you tell the truth. Your spouse or lover does not automatically have to be at the top of the list. Once again, don't leave it lying around!

EXERCISE: *Walking backwards*

This is an extremely powerful exercise that does not require a pencil or paper. Do it in your head, every day if you can, and you will be doing your psychic abilities the world of good.

The idea is to remember backwards. Start from the present moment and trace the events of the day backwards to the moment you got up.

It sounds very easy, but you try it! Remember, recall it all backwards. You will find you can remember things in sequence forwards easily enough, starting from getting up through all the events of the day until this moment. But starting from now and working back is a different thing.

People who have had near-death experiences, such as almost drowning, or an electric shock, say that their entire life flashes backwards before them in this way, from the moment of death through to the day they were born. I doubt you will get back that far, but try hard and see what you can remember. Most people soon get stuck, and find that they have to go back a chunk and then work forwards to unstick themselves.

Remember, this is a very powerful way of stimulating your mind, so don't overdo it. As you think backwards, don't push yourself too hard. You'll probably only manage it in 5 to 10 second bursts at first. A mere 10 seconds every now and again is quite enough for psychic purposes.

EXERCISE: *Four levels*

A simple, thinking exercise — no writing required. Do it anywhere, any time.

1 *Choose a day-to-day, simple, practical object. Preferably one that you can see in front you, and have some connection with. Say you choose . . . the car (which I happen to be able to see parked*

outside at the moment). The point of the exercise is to get
yourself to think about the car on four different planes or levels.

Think about *that* particular car you can see. Think of all the things
you can about that car. For example, remember the time you drove
it too fast coming in to the garage. Remember the time you bought
new seat covers for it. Reflect on its colour and the day you bought
it. In short, generally concern yourself with thoughts about this one
particular car and its associations.

2 *Now move on to the second level. Think of cars in general. Cars*
that you have seen and liked, or disliked. Big cars, small cars.
Cars that stick in your memory. The history of cars. In fact all
thoughts of cars; all cars everywhere!

3 *The third level takes you away from cars themselves, into*
thinking about what cars do. What sort of activity they cause.

I think cars are basically all about transporting people and things
from A to B (you may have other ideas). So now I think of driving
and any associations that go with it, such as seeing new places,
having freedom, the cost of having a car to drive around in,
disorientation, destruction to the environment and so on. It's not
the thing itself you think about, but what it does.

4 *Finally, the fourth level. Think of the most abstract principle*
behind the car. What quality cars have in the broadest, most
cosmic, universal way.

Really reach out and be grand. As I see it, the car is a thing of movement. Movement is its main feature. So I let my thoughts go toward
movement in the broadest possible sense. Immediately I think of
the wind, and the movement of trees (you may think of something
totally different of course). From there, I recall the feeling of
walking, and moving my body, also the movement of colours as they
flash by me when I walk fast down a crowded street. I think of things
that don't move, such as stones and rocks, or mountains. In other
words, I think of the movement idea as much as I can.
    That's all there is to it. Experiment with your own chosen
subjects and see what you come up with.

EXERCISE: *There are places*

Most of us have a place, a certain area where we spend most of our time. Usually it is the area around our home, and the local town or shops which we visit regularly. If we have lived on our patch for a while we will know it well. We will be familiar with different streets, shops, playgrounds, benches, trees, and all the other parts that we pass through regularly.

The idea of this exercise is to decide which places you like and which places you don't like. Scan through your mind as if you were going on an imaginary walk around your territory. You will find that certain parts of it leave you with a good impression and others with a not so good, or perhaps even unpleasant feeling. It is a subtle thing, but it always happens. Some places are good and some places aren't so good. The interesting thing about this exercise is that when you've decided where the good and bad places are, you will find that often they are not located at any clear cut landmark or particularly special spot. For example, a small section of one street just before you get to the park may somehow be 'not good' to you. Another corner of the same street, where the road bends to turn into the big house at the end however, may be 'good'. You don't need to give reasons. In fact, definitely don't look for reasons. Simply wander around your area in your imagination and decide which are the 'good' places and which are the 'bad'.

Some people say that the differences in the feel of various places is due to 'earth currents' and lines of force and energy running through the planet. Others say that what you are experiencing is a kind of deep primitive memory, that works by association with the land. Yet others say it is simply that at some time earlier, when you were at a certain spot, you happened to think a particularly nice or sad thought, and what you are recalling is a memory of your feeling of that moment. More of this later. For now just try to decide which places you like and which you don't like.

Talk to someone else about your opinions. You will be surprised how often your feelings, good or bad, for the most obscure places, coincide with other people's.

By now you are probably getting a bit fed up with all this thinking. So far, you have looked at the way you use your time, and examined the kind of thoughts you think. You have listed your friends, and decided which ones you most prefer. You've studied the daily objects around you and had high flown thoughts about them. And finally, you've come to some conclusions about what you like and do not like about the town where you live! All in all, you have had a good look around you. I hope the effect of all this thinking and looking has been along the following lines.

To give you practical experience and awareness that there is an 'out there' and 'in here'. These exercises help to clarify and organize the details of your daily life. They help to make the world around you more real, bring you in closer contact with it, and in so doing should solidify your 'out there' experience.

But by their very nature, these exercises will also arouse your perception of 'in here' factor in your life. Inside your head should start to become a very real and clearly defined place to you, should make itself known to you more than ever. You should be able to feel this active and thinking thing as something with an existence of its own, separate from the world outside, and separate from the thoughts and ideas that it is processing. Once you have noticed this 'thing' inside yourself you are well on your way to laying a firm foundation on which your clairvoyant abilities can safely and quickly grow.

In your psychic growth, it is very important that you stay down-to-earth. That is why the exercises concerned with your daily life, feelings and surrounds are so essential at first. Many people see clairvoyance as a 'heightened' form of awareness, and in one sense it is. If your mind is in 'high' places, you will definitely have a more intense and vivid psychic experience than if you are feeling 'low'. But remember this: the higher you want to go, the more important it is that you are rooted well into the earth.

The awakening of something inside your head that thinks about the world around it, but is not actually out there *in* the world, is important. This 'thing' is where your future lies. It is here that your clairvoyant powers will start to show themselves. You must develop a good understanding of this 'thing' and understand clearly the fact that it is separate from all the other thoughts and feelings that come flooding in from outside through your senses. Get the feel of it, and know it. It is your gateway into a new dimension. From now on, you are going to develop a whole new way of perceiving. This new way will have as its centre, not the sights and sounds of the sense world, but the subtle, slumbering feeling of the 'thing' within, just beginning to stir inside your mind. Perhaps you could begin to call it 'me'!

2
A NEW WAY OF LOOKING

This is where the fun begins. It's time to peel off a few of those layers of learning that have kept you psychically under-active for so long. But first, a few words about how to approach the psychic state of mind, and then some exercises.

Have you ever wondered why little children are so appealing? One reason, I think, is because they are so completely wrapped up in themselves. When they are happy, they laugh out loud, whether anyone else thinks it is appropriate or not! When they are upset, they cry just as loudly, and it is of little use to try to reason their unhappiness away. You and I were like that once. Quite naturally, we grew out of that stage as time went by. In this chapter we are going to take a few steps towards growing back into it.

Psychic awareness is as old as the human race (which actually isn't that old compared to many other things around on this planet). As long as there have been humans there has been the faculty of clairvoyance and the whole tradition of psychic knowledge is as relevant today as it ever was. The human mind has grown over the ages just like a child's. In our modern world we see things in a very mature, calculating and detached way. But people have not always looked at life that way. We are told that men are descended from apes; we are also told that we have evolved from creatures in the sea. Scientists and other experts have explained how the mind works, what causes disease, how nature works and so on. We are told in a mature, logical and scientific way, and we have to accept it. But no matter how expert a person seems, it must always be remembered that what they are expressing is just a point of view. The theory of evolution is just that − only a theory. Our modern views on how the body works, and what makes our minds tick, are all founded on no more than attempts by very clever people to explain what they perceive. Like the belief that the world is flat, one day they may all be superseded.

One could well ask: 'If there are so many learned and well argued theories to be found in books, why is it that so many of the writers contradict each other completely. Why, no matter how objective they are trying to be, do they all look at exactly the same things, and come to totally different conclusions?'

In psychic matters there are no hard certainties. So let us take a few bold steps into the realm of opinion. The place within us where logic doesn't rule so much, and where what counts is what we think or feel about things.

When we were children we had a childish way of looking at things. Although it was good to grow out of it, there was never any need to forget it altogether. It will be very useful for us psychically now, if we can begin to return to that dreamy, self-absorbed childish state that was once the only state of mind we knew.

A good starting point is to draw on some of the ancient traditional ideas on psychic matters. It is reassuring to know that we are not the first to take this journey. People have been experiencing, writing and talking about the psychic way for thousands of years.

Some of these ancient ideas may seem 'out of date' or quite simply ignorant or 'wrong', if you insist on looking at them in a mature twentieth-century way. But they definitely are not so; they are a simpler way of seeing. Remember, the emphasis is on what you feel about something rather than what it is supposed to be, or how it fits in with anything else. This is the most important point in this chapter. As far as you as a psychic are concerned, the whole world revolves around you. The whole show, from morning through until bedtime, from the patterns on your wallpaper to the news of events in far off lands, is all put there for one reason only: to be seen by you. It's solely for your benefit. Begin to feel free to think anything you like about anything that comes in front of you, and realize that the only reason it is in front of you is for you to have opinions about it!

Modern ways of looking at things are much too complicated to leave us much room for opinions; today, there are so many different aspects to everything that it's really rather sad. Nearly always, the need to get it exactly right robs us of the ability to have a simple opinion of our own. For example, we have learned to respond to a thunderstorm by calculating how long it will be until the noise arrives after the lightning flash, and from there to deduce that sound and light travel at different speeds. Fair enough, but there are other ways of responding. For example, we could decide whether or not we liked the noise of thunder. We could perhaps join in with it or just feel our fear of it. We could sense where in our bodies we felt the noise, and where the fear. We could ask what, or even who, was making such a noise and wonder what their feelings were! Perhaps not a very objective series of reactions, but certainly a rich starting point for exploring natural perceptions.

Or take the business of the stars, the planets and the earth's place in the heavens. It is all too easy for us to pity the people of ancient times for their ignorance about such things. Fancy, believing that the sun went around the earth! Everyone now knows that the opposite is true. But hold on. As far as a child or a simple mind is concerned, the sun *does* go around the earth. The sun 'wakes up' every morning, crosses the sky, from left to right, then goes down on the other side leaving us in darkness until it reappears again, back in the same place that it started from. No one ever sees it creeping back at night to its starting point, in preparation for the next days journey. So the only 'sensible' conclusion is that it must have gone down over the edge, around and back up the other side. You could argue that knowing the scientific facts of the matter is really no great advantage. As far as a simple enjoyment of day, night, the earth and the sun, it makes no difference what goes around what! The sun is hot, the day is bright, night follows regularly and, sure enough, the morning dawns again in all its glory as expected. What could be simpler? Life is in no way improved by knowing the scientific truth of the situation. The facts might well even spoil our enjoyment of the world. And that is what has happened to many of us. We carry around in our heads a lot of rigid learning that we don't really understand in our hearts.

The Elements: Fire, Air, Water, Earth

So how are we to look at the world around us simply and safely, in order to enhance our psychic awareness? Well, as far as nurturing clairvoyance is concerned, the old ways are undoubtedly best. They are looser, and more likely to stimulate a feeling of involvement. This is essential; you have got to be drawn in to what is around you. A scientist looking down a microscope may see a great deal. His notebook will doubtless contain reams of information on what he has seen. But it is very unlikely that there will be one word about what he feels about what he has seen. That is what we will start to do now.

In order to help you begin to start forming new, looser opinions I shall now present to you the older view of the world. I had better

God-made and man-made

add that I will no longer be apologizing for this view, or referring to it as 'old' or 'ancient' to help its credibility in a sceptical world. It is, in fact, a perfectly valid and extremely useful way of looking at your surroundings and your own place in them . . . valid that is if you want to develop your psychic perceptions! So try to accept, absorb and enjoy it.

The world around you is divided into two distinct parts. If you know which part is which you can cut down by half any complications in your psychic life! One half of the world is made by God, and the other half is made by Man. Or, if you prefer to think of it another way. One half is made by Man, and the other half by Nature.

Look around you right now. How much of what you see is natural and how much is man-made? If you're a city dweller, you will probably find that the balance is heavily on the side of man-made. In fact most of our lives (city or country dwellers) are dominated by man-made objects, events, and situations. This dominance of man-made and inspired things in our lives, is probably the one single factor that has contributed most to our present, limited psychic development. Psychic abilities are an entirely natural phenom-enon. They grow, live and move entirely in natural things. You simply do not find the necesssary inspiration for clairvoyant perception in most man-made objects and situations. There was an age when you did, but that has long passed into pre-history. So, it is important to understand that the place to look for the first encouraging stirrings of your psychic abilities is exclusively in the world of natural things.

For many people, simply having the difference pointed out is a turning point. It starts in their mind an extremely powerful process of selection. Their latent psychic drive immediately siezes on the idea, and a most satisfying urge to discriminate begins.

It is as if some deeper part of you has at last found a formula for selecting only those things that it can feed on. One simple thought can filter out what is good for your psychic growth from what has little or nothing to give it. Natural things have an altogether cleaner cut and more easy to perceive 'feel'. Natural or man-made? That is the first way of getting closer to the psychic sources within you.

To loosen up the psychic function you must have a simple way of answering within yourself this simple question:

'What is this I see in front of me?'

That may sound a bit vague, so let me explain further. Modern science has listed 109 naturally occurring elements; and research has discovered that everything in this world is made out of one or more of these materials. This is indisputably true, but it is of little use to ordinary folk as a yardstick for looking at the world around us. We need to use a simpler, more 'human' way of understanding what comes before our senses. For psychic purposes, there is another very beautiful and magical way of seeing everything.

All the things in your life and in the world around, whether made by Man or God (nature), are made up of one of four elements.

Although science has moved on to a more complex understand-ing, this rule which was true thousands of years ago can still be applied today. Knowing it can be a tremendous help in organizing your impressions of life. Seeing things in these terms brings with it the beginnings of a new psychic way of enjoying life.

To grasp the feeling of the four elements may take a little time, and a sympathetic approach. The underlying feeling behind fire,

air

water, earth, and air, is extremely broad, but rich, natural to the mind and very rewarding. Get to know it well.

Obviously, there is no scientific proof of the theory of the four elements. None is possible and none is needed. It stands or falls on the simple statement that everything in the whole universe is made up of fire, air, earth or water. The idea is for you to grasp the essential feel of each element on its own, and then to look for that feeling in all the other things in your life.

One of the main advantages of this simple system of perceiving, is that it includes you, the person who is perceiving. The elements include you. Try this exercise immediately: Stop for just a second and look for the elements of earth, water, air, and fire in your own body.

I don't know what ideas you will have come up with after such a short pause, but surely the following must be true. Our human body is simply a bag of warm liquid, with air flowing in and out. It can be looked at as a package with a small mineral content, a huge fluid content (about 75 per cent of the total weight), with air and gasses entering and circulating within it. What is more, it is hot all over. It obeys all the rules that all the other elements are subject to. In short, if you know about them, you will know about you.

Obviously commonsense demands that you don't interpret the words 'earth' as brown soily substance, 'fire' as flickering yellow tongues in a grate, and so on. Even as you read the words you must begin to look for the broader feelings that underly each element. Here are some guidelines to start you off.

Fire

The first, most basic element. A gift from the gods some say. The power that set men apart from animals was their ability to use fire. Warmth. The source of fire is the sun, a heavenly ball of flame so hot it warms the whole earth, and everyone on it. Fire is the purest and oldest of the elements. Without heat there is no life. Fire is in everything that is warm, everything that shines and sparkles. All feelings that burn or flare up, that smoulder or simmer, are fiery feelings.

Look at actual fires that burn around you in daily life. This is most important. Even the flicker in the central heating boiler has a magic potential. You can see how the bright flame, bursts forth alive and hot behind the glass when the heating turns on. How vibrant it looks compared to the solid metal surrounding it. Fire is the most alive element. No fire, no life.

Learn to appreciate this element, because fire is in every living thing to a greater or lesser extent. If you learn to recognize the feeling of fire in yourself you will soon be able to recognize it in others. Fire changes things. It breaks some things down and con-sumes others, converting them into itself. It demands feeding or it fades away. If it *is* fed, it moves outward to meet what is around it. Fire is dynamic, and active and can always be dangerous and destructive.

Once again, look carefully at any flames, sparks, hotplates, furnaces, internal combustions and so on that you meet in daily life. Natural or man made, all contain fire at their core. Fire is always natural. Fire cannot be synthesized; fire is always fire. Colour comes from the sun's fire. All colour and light has more or less fire in it. Some colours are hot, others are cool or even cold. All nature is ablaze with colour.

Later, I will be going in to much more detail on how to use natural objects to quicken our psychic responses. For now, all you have to do is to accept the idea of the existence of the element of fire and begin to notice it around you. In this way you will develop a feel within your self for the 'fire' feeling.

Air

There is a story about a young fish who went to the head of his school and asked: 'What is this "water" that everyone keeps talking about?' The senior fish, realizing that the youngster had been born in water, lived in water, was surrounded on all sides at all times by water, and was actually made of ninety-eight per cent water, found it very hard to give a satisfactory reply!

Writing about water may seem a strange way of introducing the air element, but the moral of the tale is that most of us have probably never really noticed air before, despite the fact that it is literally everywhere. Stop and think about it. At least, with water, the first thing you can say about it is it's wet! What is the first thing you can say about air? Ask someone to talk about air, and they will often be reduced to opening and closing their mouths and gasping 'um, um', looking not unlike fishes!

Air is the next purest element after fire. The sun blazes, out in the heavens. Beneath the sun is air. Air is weightless and quick moving. Always in motion, it changes direction at a moment's notice. It comes and goes in and out of our bodies and is our breath. Although it is invisible, it is the carrier of the most powerful psychic sense . . . sound. Music, harmony and rhythm are carried to us on the element, air. Our own voice is the result of trying to mould and form this slippery element. Air is the carrier of communication and speech, and inspires thought.

All things that are light and rise up, disappear into the air, and there is nothing more subtle than this element. Air brings us news of things we cannot see. Our ears, and most importantly our sense of smell, are subtle receptors in a 'sea' of air.

Get to know the feel of air. One of its major properties is its ability to make us think, strange as that may sound. Picture the following scene.

A man and a woman are lazing drowsily in a peaceful landscape. Suddenly, there is a change in the atmosphere. Just as suddenly, their minds are awakened from their pleasant dozing. They look up, full of questions. Is that burning? What is on fire? Where? They have literally got wind of something, and their minds are now on full alert and racing! (Actually, it was all all right in the end; their house wasn't burning down. It was the neighbour's bonfire.) Whatever way you look at it, air is the vehicle for a lot of the more abstract things of life.

The weather comes to us courtesy of the air. It is toward the wind and the clouds that we will probably start to look for the 'air' feeling first. A good start is to watch the shapes of the clouds and try to see creatures and objects in the changing forms. The feel of air is very present in this activity. At first, you will also probably only notice air when it gets violent, when you can feel it on your skin, or when it starts to move things like dustbin lids, TV aerials or roof tiles. Air can be very strong, and it has a mischievous and unco-operative side. Try carrying home a big sheet of hardboard, or wearing a hat on a blustery day and you will soon be made aware of air's abilities to be troublesome!

Trees, too, are a great help to us in seeing thin air and how it moves. Trees are very much objects of the air, even though their makeup is much denser.

Also, casually watch the patterns of rising smoke, or the steam from your coffee cup.

Water

Beneath the sun, beneath the air, water lives. An ocean of liquid embracing solid rock. Denser than air, but not as rigid as earth. The element water remains unformed and open to influences . . . a bit wet and wishy-washy!

Left to itself, water will form a perfect globe, just like the planet it enfolds. Normally it oscillates around the shape of a sphere, or takes on whatever shape it is offered. Water is always ready to receive. It is solid enough to be subject to gravity, and will always try to seek out a lower place. It tends downwards with a vengeance, and always seems to want to be somewhere else!

Perhaps you will sense a personal, almost human touch in the way I am describing water. Water tries to flow around and join together. It mixes happily with air and with earth, and can move huge quantities of these sharply opposed elements. It circulates and carves the ground it flows over in rhythmic curves. It can make itself light enough to be carried up into the air to paint the sky with the sparkling curves of a rainbow. (On a summer's day, from just one single acre of woodland, 3,500 gallons of water evaporate into the air.)

Water can be very emotional. Deep and powerful, it conceals a mysterious world beneath its rippling surface. It also has huge momentum and can be devastating when roused. Get caught by the tide, or fall into a river, and you will soon experience the ruthless strength of water. But most of the time, the feeling of this element is rich and fruitful. There is always a hint of conflict in the way water wobbles between being the perfect globule it wants to be, and the shapes that gravity forces on to it. It has an irresistible and very physical, rhythmic motion; it comes and goes inevitably, with the tides and the seasons, and in many other ways. Water was always thought to be very humble. It not only changes shape, it also changes its very substance to accommodate. In its natural cycle, it circulates from liquid, through vapour or ice, back to liquid again (a cycle which it repeats about 34 times in a year). Whether rushing to the sea in a torrent, or tumbling to the earth as snow, water has always got somewhere to go.

Water carries life, and teems with rich shapes and forms. As I have said before, water is the human element. No matter how solid you may feel, remember that you are 75 per cent water. The human foetus rests in a sac of water (amniotic fluid) until birth . . . Tears are a good starting point for getting to know the water feelings. House plants too, are another watery species. How susceptible they are to what is around them. In some of them you can actually see the water rising and falling within the almost transparent stem.

Water has a playful side that seals, dolphins, and otters are so imbued with. Clowns with buckets of water, and all the splashy games of childhood epitomize this wet sense of fun too.

The moon, ruler of the tides, has great power over all water ideas and feelings. I will be going into more detail about the effect of the moon on budding psychic abilities later. For now, just imagine the effect that such a mighty, ocean-moving force can have on creatures who are mostly water. The human brain actually floats suspended in water, protected in a sea of cranial fluid.

Water is magic. Underwater, heavy things become light. Scatter water on barren ground and life springs up. Mix water with dyes and colours can miraculously appear and transform themselves. Sprinkle water liberally over dirty objects, and hey presto . . . they are clean again.

Look out for water wherever you go, it is a much misunderstood and avoided element, but deep down, it means no harm!

Earth

By now you are probably getting a feel for the elements. From the highest and most rarefied (some might say the most spiritual) fire, we move slowly towards the denser air (mental?), on through the heavier though as yet undecided water (emotional?) and finally to the firm and fixed material kingdom of the earth (physical). I must stress that this is *not* a list in order of importance, or preference, or anything else like that. It is perhaps more like a journey if you want to look at it that way.

If you find you do have a distinct preference for, or an aversion to any one element, it would be best at this stage to try to leave that opinion behind. All elements are equal and locked together in perfect harmony. To have favourites at this stage would throw you slightly out of balance. So try to appreciate all the different feelings the elements bring into your life, and let your observation of them be fair.

This brings us to earth, where we spend most of our time in this material plane. Earth moves slowest, lasts longest, and resists change. Earth is rock and minerals and is definitely here for ever. All the other elements come to rest on solid earth and, in a way, earth is the end of the journey. Water may be rich but earth is richer. Earth is more generous too, slowly forming and reforming all the shapes of the animal, vegetable and mineral kingdom. All the ideas and rhythms of air, and the movements of water actually become real thanks to solid Mother Earth. If you think about it, even the light from the fiery sun owes earth a debt. Believe it or not, light itself is invisible! It is only when light strikes something solid that you know it is there. The space between the sun and the earth is filled with light, streaming inwards, but you can't see it until it touches the hardness of earth.

The mineral world is to all intents and purposes motionless, because it does not have a rhythm that can be felt in a single lifespan. Without the intervention of written records, and a lot of mental activity, the mineral kingdom appears unchanging and un-changeable. Gold and silver, mountains and stones, wood and bone, all have the earth element foremost in them.

But it is not so easy to get the true feel of the earth element, for all its solidity. The harder you try, the more elusive it becomes. It takes a little practice. Material objects seem to resist showing the qualities that are uniquely their own. Instead, things of earth are more likely to bounce back whatever feelings you unconsciously project on to them. Because of this it is very easy to be fascinated, even enchanted, by earth objects . . . you're really looking at yourself. They generously return with interest whatever feelings or opinions you care to put on to them. This is very gratifying but also somehow a bit narcissistic. It means you rarely actually see this element for what it is!

In the human, the sense of touch is a starting point for knowing earth. Textures of all kinds help awaken earth appreciation. Pressure, weight and huge old items of furniture that you can't budge an inch are all to do with earth: More subtly, the feel of different fabrics is an earth sensation too. For example, the difference between wool and acrylic. Many people will not wear artificial fibres because of the difference they feel. Man-made velvets and silks are another example. These are solid, earth-based materials, which can look very attractive, yet have a 'different' quality which makes them unacceptable to some. That kind of appreciation is an understanding of the earth element. Food and taste are also earth sensations.

Our watery body is contained in a solid, earthy shell by this element. We have in our bones and teeth exactly the same minerals that are lying around on the ground outside right now. Not forgetting the metals and crystals found throughout our body. A list of them reads like an inventory of a chemical works: sulphur, chalk, iron, iodine, salt, copper (no brass!), lime, carbon and so on. All this we owe to earth.

In a way, metals are the best starting point for appreciating the true feel of this imposing but shy element of earth, especially as it can be felt in your body. Most of us have a natural liking for one or other metal which, if we can learn to get in touch with it a bit more intensely, will lead on to a wider appreciation. At first, some people feel nothing for metals, but are fascinated by wood, paper or perhaps stone. Earth is definitely in these things too, and waiting patiently to be discovered, so do experiment.

Now that you have a general introduction to the elements, here are some exercises.

It would not be practical to make these exercises too specific, as what you are trying to do is develop a much looser way of looking at your life, and the things around you. Later, when we get to more specialized techniques, the exercises will be more clear-cut. It would do you no good to make an inner decision to 'go out and see the world in terms of the four elements' or to 'be more subjective' or some similar aim. Instead, simply let any ideas that have caught your interest rise up in your mind whenever they like. This will be most beneficial.

The following games are offered in a spirit of fun, to encourage the desirable, more childish perceptions from which your psychic abilities can begin to grow.

Exercise: Cooking

Cooking is a very basic activity many of us do every day. However, next time you are in the kitchen, look at what is around you and what you are doing, in terms of the elements. It may seem a little mad at first, but don't worry, try to get into this kind of approach. Here are a few guidelines.

1 *Gas or electric, ceramic hob, charcoal grill or camping stove, whichever you have in front of you, the element is fire. Fire is at the centre of what you are about to do. You can see it brighter than everything else, red or blue (unless it's in direct sunshine, of course).*

2 *The fire is going to change the hard, earthy food into something softer. With luck, the fire might even enhance the earth food and make it taste better. You can control the fire, but it will need careful watching; it will not hesitate to burn and destroy your meal if you do not stay vigilant. Fire has a quick will of its own.*

3 *Pans full of bubbling water send steam up into the air. But first, what are pans made of? Steel, aluminium, copper. How do you feel about your pans?*

Do you wish you had more solid copper ones? (I do). How do you feel about the plastic coating on your new frying pan? Strange questions perhaps, but sure to bring answers about earth feelings.

4 *Watch the steam as it rises. Air has no fixed shape, but it does form regular patterns. Watch the surface of the water as it gives off steam to the air.*

Once again, there will be no fixed shape but definite forms in the flow. Does the steam in the air move like the water in the pan? One goes up and disappears while the other goes round and round. Remember, you are still cooking a meal, so don't get too carried away! If you do happen to spill something on to your cooker, watch how the heat drives out the liquid element from the spill. When the liquid dries, the now solid (earth) stain will still hold a curving, watery shape. With a bit of imagination those splatter marks can become fascinating!

5 *The food you chop is a mixture of elements. Hard fibres and juices. Watch how you cut certain foods. It usually tells you something about the movement of the forces that formed that particular vegetable.*

Do you get the idea? I have always been a bit eccentric so this all reads perfectly normally to me. People have said that I look like an ancient alchemist when I cook. I often feel like one, standing in front of my crusted old iron gas cooker, turning the flames up and down, getting it all just right. With all the bubbling and gurgling noises and the swirling and stirring and tasting it is positively magic! Make what you can of cooking, there is plenty to experience 'elementally'.

EXERCISE: *Observing*

Here is an activity to encourage you to begin to feel free to form sweeping statements about people and things in your own mind and make grand sounding conclusions from small inner impressions. Once again, this is an element exercise and best done outdoors over a period of time rather than in a deliberate head-on way.

People are intensely drawn to fire, water, earth, and air, but they don't know it. The idea of this exercise is to go out and see for yourself.

1 *If you notice a man fishing by a pond, watch him for a while.*

The only conclusion you will be able to reach is that this man is in love with water! You will find he is in a kind of gentle trance, nurturing an obviously intense underlying desire for fish! He is showing qualities of water.

2 *Carry on observing and you will find many other watery things going on around, and in the behaviour of your fisherman.*

People love to involve themselves closely with elements outdoors:

Kite flyers   Bulldozer drivers
Bonfire   Gardeners
Ball players   Sun bathers

water   *earth*

The list is literally endless. Step outside and see who is doing what with what element.

3 *A further refinement of this exercise is to ask yourself, 'Do they love the element they are playing with, or do they hate it?'*

No sitting-on-the-fence verdicts permitted! Also, don't come to any negative, hostile or disrespectful conclusions about anyone you see. Be friendly and simply *see*.

EXERCISE: *Shouting back*

This is an easy, nonsense game to be played only for a few seconds, or a minute at the most. It helps you to get the necessary momentum up to voice completely unfounded statements! Obviously, this is *not* psychic ability in any form whatsoever, but this little game will loosen something up within you that could help later on in your growth.

1 *Turn on the radio or TV to a station where someone is talking. It doesn't matter what they are talking about.*

2 *Now, disagree out loud on every point they make.*

If they say it is two-thirty on a Wednesday afternoon, deny it immediately, and insist that it is three-thirty-five on a Thursday morning! If they say it's sunny and the traffic is moving freely . . . refuse to believe it, and state loudly that the roads are jammed to a standstill, and the rain is falling harder than it has done for decades. Find as many points as possible to contradict on and keep arguing relentlessly.

3
SOME PRACTICAL STEPS

In this fascinating business of helping you to unfold your psychic abilities, the one thing you are up against at first is impatience. Your interest may have been aroused by all the exciting, traditional techniques of clairvoyance, such as hearing voices, seeing auras, predicting the future with cards or with any of a thousand and one other fascinating means of divining. Crystal balls, psychometric readings, automatic writing, thought projection, and a lot more besides will all have doubtless captured your imagination at some time, and quite rightly. So who could blame you for wanting to get on with it.

Get on with it we will, rest assured. All the above subjects will become a part of your life if you should so desire, as a result of following the guidance given in this book. You will be able to practise whichever one or ones you feel a natural talent for whenever you want. But do understand the broader meaning of your psychic abilities. Concentration too soon on the traditional techniques of psychic practice will limit you a lot and most probably leave you with very little psychic experience at all after a few months. The 'recipe book' approach to this magical and intensely personal subject simply doesn't work.

Let me explain. If I were to merely give you a list of 'do's and don'ts' on, for example, how to read tea-leaves, or the crystal ball, you would probably get up from your first reading more confused than when you sat down. I'm sure you have had the experience of trying to cook a dish from a recipe that was too complicated. It all looks so simple on paper, but when you come to do it, nothing goes half as smoothly as you feel it should. You start wondering whether perhaps you should have done step two a little more this way or that way, but never mind, you plough ahead anyway, until you reach that dreadful point when the recipe asks you to do something that is totally impossible, given the creation you have in front of you! Obviously, the idea was to produce something completely different . . . but where did it go wrong? That is a sad feeling and definitely one to be avoided if possible.

It must be said also that the techniques of actual clairvoyant performance are few. Eventually, everybody practises the psychic art largely in their own way, when it comes down to the details. This coupled with the fact that there are many people of small natural psychic ability who are only too ready to clothe what they do in a welter of mumbo jumbo, makes the explaining of psychic abilities a delicate and subtle matter, most unsuited to a heavy handed 'do this, then that, and hey presto results are guaranteed' approach.

To achieve results psychically is possible, and I will show you, but it depends more on what you are than on what you do.

In this chapter I will explain something about the nature of clair-voyance, and how it is best practised at first, in order to lay as solid a basis as possible for its full blossoming as you go on. Then I will suggest specific exercises for you to try at your leisure.

What is the point of clairvoyance? Most of us are attracted to psychic growth by curiosity about our own potential, rather than any deep-seated desire to become a practising medium or psychic. Very few of those who read this book will become regular practitioners or consultants. Yet nearly all of what comes to our ears on these matters concerns a tiny few who are highly developed in the business of dispensing psychic advice, and solve the problems of others by means of specialized and usually genuine clairvoyant powers.

We could be forgiven for assuming that to be psychic is to have the answers to other people's problems, and to be the possessor of great wisdom about many things. This is not so. Knowing about other people and their affairs is only one form of psychism. It is one that evolves quite naturally as a result of first practising a much more common and easy-going psychic pursuit . . . using psychic powers to learn about yourself. And it is this that I am going to emphasize, before proceeding to explain the traditional techniques.

If you have read and done even a few of the exercises so far in this book, you are already likely to find that you have perceptibly deeper understanding of the world about you. As a person who seeks to un-fold your hidden powers, you are already in a position to consider just what it is you want to do with your new abilities. Before going further, ask yourself if you are really ready yet to put yourself in the position of oracle. At this early stage, do you really want to have people asking you for advice on their problems, on the outcome for them if they do this or that? You might soon find your enthusiasm a little dampened by the responsibility if you do. So, for now, try to develop your psychic insight for your own benefit, rather than seek out specific facts about worldly matters to help others.

Clairvoyance is of two basic sorts, each causing you to use and feel widely different feelings. One type contains a 'time' element, and can leave you feeling quite drained if you do it successfully. Some mediums, particularly the trance mediums of the early part of this century, often ended their sessions in a sweaty state of near collapse! (An extreme phenomenon, not going to be recommended, and not necessary.)

'Time Clairvoyance', is prophecy and divination of possible futures; days, months or years ahead, sometimes reaching beyond this lifetime. It is also the act of looking psychically backwards, into both the recent past and further back, into the time before birth and into past lifetimes. It is the mystery of predicting the future, and gaining information about the past. It is the area of psychic activity that receives the most attention, and it is also the area that requires the most careful handling and experience to practise. We will be dealing with it later.

Type two, is clairvoyance with NO time component. In my experience it always feels uplifting and exhilarating. It is this second type of clairvoyance that I intend to start you off with. It is incidently by far the more powerful and far reaching.

What we are going to pursue is called Psychic Insight . . . that area of psychic activity that has no time component. It deals with the psychic perception of ourselves and the world around us, and provides a rich source of natural growth for all budding clairvoyants. It is an entirely personal phenomenon, with profound, 'eye opening' side effects, and one that you can use in your daily life without taking on the responsibility of answering other people's questions and doubts about the future. That comes later.

How to gain psychic insight? The first step is to abandon words and ideas as your main way of thinking.

Imagination

The key to developing psychic insight is your imagination. For most of us who are new to psychic experience, the word imagination probably conjures up associations that make us wonder how such a vague and unreal thing as 'imagination' can be so important. But at this stage it is your imagination first and foremost that can take you on your first psychic adventures. These adventures will not be unreal or 'imaginary' by any means; they will be extremely practical.

Most of us are hardly aware that we have a faculty of imagination. It is almost completely neglected. No-one at school ever mentioned our imagination, except perhaps in art lessons where a gifted few were said to have 'vivid' ones and the rest of us were judged not to have any at all! Even those who had vivid ones were regarded as dreamers, or slightly hopeless cases who couldn't be expected to deal with the real world that the rest of us inhabited. Imagination was seen as a refuge from what was actually real, solid, and meaningful. Most of us probably left whatever education we had with the assumption bred in us that imagination was only indulged in by people who were hiding from the serious business of getting on with the hard facts of life. How untrue! Imagination plays a key part in nearly everything we do. It is a natural human sense, and it needs training.

Imagination is the ability to picture in our heads things that are not visible around us. It is a faculty we possess to make an image inside ourselves of whatever we want, rather than what is put upon us by the outside world. In no sense need it be a retreat from the practical world. Many a businessperson has started off the most far reaching money-making scheme as a result of having one clear picture in their mind of the way things could be.

Picture the scene! Suddenly, after a hard day of selling hot potatoes, the humble street vendor sees a derelict shop! In a flash, he pictures it renovated and 'done up', with himself inside surrounded by new tables covered by white linen tablecloths. On them the wine glasses sparkle, while dozens of smartly dressed diners eat his immaculately cooked food, chattering and laughing. He pictures the bar in the back, and a chandelier hanging in the centre, where now there is only brick and broken plaster. Consciously he says to himself 'I wonder if that place would make a good restaurant?' Several months later he finds himself asking a friend to lend him some money to try out a 'business idea' he thinks might prove to be a 'practical proposition'. And the project is underway.

Or perhaps you know the feeling of mentally seeing a room in your house decorated in a certain way. You have a clear impression of how you want it. The walls in light greeny blue, textured paper on the ceiling, and shapely glass lamp fittings in the alcove. In your imagination it is all there. But then you go out to buy the paint, the paper and the lights. Can you find them? No. Nowhere. You tramp the length and breadth of the town in the rain, bumping into other shoppers and having endless complicated conversations with sales people! Suddenly, as the traffic warden gleefully sticks his ticket on your car, or you wait for your bus home in the rain, you realize just what it was that got you into this very real experience. It was your imagination. One little picture in your head started the whole thing off. For better or worse, the power of your imagination played its part.

A very real force

All this is not intended to get you to go out and set up restaurants or avoid amateur interior designing. It is simply to point out that imagination is a very real force, possessed by all of us. And it is a force to be reckoned with. It is a function that we use quite practically when we want to, and we can develop this mysterious faculty as we wish.

Strengthening your imagination is the way toward psychic insight for the moment. Let me tell you very clearly and simply what is the key to coming to grips with the imagination. The key is pictures and images. Visual symbols and shapes are vital to stimulating inner growth. To grasp imagination you must think in pictures and images. These are the language of your imagination. Words are not; they are far too 'grown up'. You have to be able to go back to a time before you learned to read and strive to create in your mind pictures. There are ways of doing this, and you will find plenty to help you in the exercises that follow.

You can expect some surprises when you deliberately awaken your picture-loving imagination in the ways recommended. There is much within us that is very exciting, and can set us wondering. Let me remind you of the message in Chapter One, and suggest you keep yourself firmly in the world of thoughts and your daily life if you intend to explore your imaginative abilities. The firmer you are fixed in the hurly burly of daily life, the easier it will be for you to let your imagination come to the surface. It may sound contradictory but it's true. The deeper into the ground your foundations are set, the higher you can build your building. Opening up your imagination by means of visual thinking is not an end in itself, it is a means of attaining clairvoyance. Imagination is the gateway to natural psychic awareness.

In this modern, western society, the only people who have made any profound attempt to explore our responses to visuals and images have been the media and advertisers of all kinds. Every day they expose us to symbols, shapes, colours, and pictures of every description. All of them have one thing in common. They have been put upon us largely for the purpose of controlling us in some way, or parting us from our money. The persuasion business has developed great insight into the human psyche and how to get at it by stimulating our imaginations with appropriate pictures. The result is that we have become desensitized to all but the most powerful images. What's more, we have come to associate visual input with a feeling that we are being manipulated in some way.

Neon lights, enormous posters, flickering cinema screens flashing scene after exotic scene in larger-than-life colour, and much much more, all contribute to deaden our inner responses. When we come to look at the contents of our own imaginations for the very first time, we are often blind to all but the most obvious visual feelings. But don't worry, it takes only a few weeks to begin to shake off the numbness that the years have imposed. The mind is extremely resilient.

Media diet

Now a rather controversial point, but one that will contribute dramatically to the growth of your psychic ability. It concerns the apparently harmless business of watching television.

If someone were to ask me what was the one single, most sure fire thing they could do to increase their psychic awareness as quickly as possible, with the least possible effort, I would say: stop watching television: Yes, watch no more TV, at all, for at least a month. The idea may seem outrageous but in my experience it is true. I do not say this for any kill-joy reasons, or because I am anti-media, or anti-anything. The fact is, that regardless of what is on television, the act of watching it is extremely destructive to the imagination. By stifling the visual imagination, TV retards the psychic powers, causing them to wither altogether or, more likely, to surface uncomfortably and sporadically.

Try this experiment, as part of your plan for psychic growth. Watch no television at all for at least a month (then preferably for evermore). You will notice some dramatic developments in your psychic life. Oh, and don't go to the cinema too often either? 'TV fasting' is a serious suggestion, but obviously one that must be seen in perspective. I do not own a TV, but out of choice, and with no feeling of sacrifice. Try this simple exercise, and see for yourself. (By the way, I go to the cinema whenever I feel like it, and so should everyone!)

Getting the imagination going

There are two main approaches to this. One is to stimulate imagination from the outside, by looking at appropriate images ... and the images do have to be of the right sort. The second is to work from the inside, creating suitable visuals within your mind.

To encourage the first stirrings of psychic awareness through visual awakening, there is no better stimulant than the Tarot. Tarot cards are an excellent starting point, regardless of whether you want to use them to tell fortunes or not. I thoroughly recommend you get your very own pack as soon as you can. If you've already got a pack, get them out and have a close look at them. Check that you actually like the design of your cards and be sure that you are not just in possession of them because you were given them or they were found lying about. The idea for our purposes is to have a pack of Tarot that you have chosen because you like the look of them.

In fact, in telling you to get your own pack I am going somewhat against tradition. Many experienced Tarot readers will tell you that to be given a Tarot pack, or simply to stumble across one, is a great good fortune. All the best Tarot packs seek out the people that they want to use them! This is quite true, but there is a difference for our purposes. I am not recommending Tarot so that we can use the cards to tell fortunes. No. There are other ways of using the Tarot pack which can lead on to much wider psychic applications.

Tarot Cards are the forerunners of modern playing cards, and consist of seventy-eight cards, divided into two groups: a fifty-six card pack, called the Minor Arcana, and a twenty-two card pack called the Tarot Trumps, or the Major Arcana. They are sold together, as one pack, but it is the cards of the major arcana that will be of the most interest to us. There are four suits in the pack. Batons, cups, swords, coins. These may be referred to by other names, e.g. rods for batons, pentacles for coins, and many other possible variations. Already, here is a lesson to be learned. Don't let the labels confuse you. A rod looks like a rod, whatever the writing on the card may say. The same goes for the other suits. Choose the pack that most appeals to you, whatever the words may say.

The strong point about Tarot is that it is a series of cards whose meanings are completely visual. They are a picture book for grownups. Today, most adult 'pictures only' books are comics and cartoons, or perhaps basic instruction leaflets, designed to elicit no more than a passing chuckle or to show you how to put your new coffee table together. The images on the Tarot inspire deeper feelings.

Perhaps when you were a child you remember experiences such as the following. Your mother, father, or some other grown-up is reading you a story. As they read you lean over and look at the picture on each page. Their voice provides a warm and comforting background, almost a drone, telling you interesting things. But the main source of your pleasure is the pictures. Your eyes wander around the page, noticing little details, and always coming back to your favourite bits. Perhaps the sun setting warmly on the hill, or the princess's golden crown. Or maybe it's the shapes of the toy cars in the corner, or the face of the angry giant peering in through the window. Whatever it is, the picture is completely real to your young eyes, and you are fascinated and totally absorbed by the feelings it evokes. For whole minutes you are not thinking, you are not talking, and after the first few readings, you are probably not even listening in any conscious way. You are living in your imagination.

Well that's the way of looking at things that you can return to with the Tarot card pictures. By looking at them over a period of time, perhaps as little as a week, you will begin to notice feelings inside yourself that are completely new, yet at the same time very familiar. This is a sign that you are beginning to make your first contact with your psychic ability.

Let me go into a little more detail about the cards. When you go to buy a pack of Tarot, you will be faced with many different designs. They will all have the basic 78 cards, in the same four suits but the pictures on them will be in completely different styles. Choose the one you like. If you go to a magical paraphernalia shop you will be able to shuffle through and see all the cards in each pack. It is best to do this if possible. Large bookshops and department stores also stock Tarot decks, but most likely the packs will be sealed in clear polythene, so you will only be able to see the one on the front. Don't worry. Once again, simply go for the pack you like the look of. However, it is worth asking to see all the cards of the pack that catches your eye, regardless of the sales assistant's possible reaction!

For our purposes, I suggest that you make your choice from the more traditional packs. In recent years a lot of new packs have appeared on the market, and some of the wilder ones might not help you. The Tarot of Cats, The Tarot of Sex, among others, and the Tarot of A. Crowley, though good in their own way, might cause you to miss the point at this early stage, so why not stay broadly traditional at first.

Having got the cards, the thing to do now is to look at them. Find a quiet space in the day, and a time when you are on your own and scan through at random. You will see before you a blaze of shapes, signs, symbols, flowers, weapons, animals, monsters, angels, bodies, suns, moons and planets.

It is an interesting fact that many newcomers to Tarot packs find them slightly frightening at first. They get a kind of a tingle in their stomach, and a sensation that they are looking at something vaguely sinister. If this happens to you on your first scanning through, all well and good. It is a sign of sensitivity on your part, so persevere and your trepidation will soon be replaced by excitement. Feelings of potential and new discovery will begin to arise in you.

Note and hold these feelings; they will be sporadic, and fade within seconds. That is natural. But do try to hold on to them long enough to get to know them a little. At least notice them enough so that you will recognize them the next time you feel them. Also notice them enough so that you can tell the difference between your new Tarot inspired feelings, and the other feelings of your daily life.

The cards that you will do best to concentrate on are the 22 scenes pictures on the major arcana. Most packs contain a leaflet to help you identify these.

The spirit in which you look at these pictures is important. You must look at them quietly and reflectively, if you want any meaning to filter through to you. The cards work by awakening symbols buried deep in your unconscious mind. These symbols somehow rise up and suddenly, as if by magic, pop into your clear thinking, day-to-day, rational mind. They bring with them some emotional content too, so be ready to feel feelings! . . . and to notice what you feel. Emotional reactions to the cards are a sign that the process is working, that the cards are getting through — via your visual imagination — to your psychic centres.

EXERCISE: Picture-book Tarot

1 *Once you have selected the cards of the major arcana, lay them out in order before you. Then simply let your eyes wander over the array before you.*

You will inevitably be drawn to certain cards. Most likely the Devil, and the Hanged Man, or the Tower. Don't let superstition get the better of you with these apparently negative images. You'll probably have to take it on faith at first but, believe me, there is nothing negative about these or any other of the Tarot pictures. They are stimulating, yes, but there is no harm in them.

2 *Select a card that you like, preferably not one of the dramatic ones. Take the card and place it where you will see it quite often every day. It requires no more of you now than to simply notice it now and again by consciously glancing at it whenever you remember.*

3 *If you wish, leave the pack laid out in any order you like, or perhaps carry it around with you and simply shuffle through it in spare moments, pausing to let your eye wander over any one image or detail that catches your eye.*

For now, that is all you need do with your Tarot pack. Just treat it like a picture book and pick it up and put it down privately, at your leisure. Results will come automatically.

Do fortunes with the cards if you want, but I really don't recommend it at this stage. If you are inexperienced, you might confuse yourself, or simply end up bluffing to appear more aware than you are but feel free to try on close friends if you must.

Later, I will show you a technique called visualization, in which the Tarot pack can be used to great effect in ·a more 'inner' imaginative way. A word of advice. Browsing through an array of twenty or so static cards may seem a little boring and you could be forgiven for getting frustrated at your lack of concentration ... especially if you are accustomed to more powerful all-singing, all-dancing, moving pictures in full colour and stereo! Don't be tricked! There is a magic psychic process at work here that you may not be aware of, so whatever you do don't let frustration get at you because you can concentrate only for a few seconds at a time. In a few seconds, a huge amount of visual learning happens. It is quite unlike the mental 'word' learning that we are so schooled in.

The experience of the few seconds we can manage to hold, absorbing Tarot images, is like the concentrated moments we spend dreaming. It is a short, compressed and highly intense form of experience. One second in a dream can seem to go on for hours, yet as you probably know, research has shown that most dreams last no more than a few seconds.

Don't be surprised to find Tarot images appearing in your dreams, either, but more about that later!

Your Tarot is your starter on the road to psychic insight. Browse through in your own way, whenever you can, and you will notice results within days.

EXERCISE: *Playing the symbols*

Symbols of all kinds surround us everywhere. They are those instantly recognizable non-verbal, attention grabbing shapes that even people who can't read can understand. Each one speaks its message so much clearer than words. 'This way to the Underground'. 'Watch out for falling stones'. 'Drive in here for a cup of tea and somewhere to sleep'. Car parks, restaurants and all modern public places abound with them.

This process of expressing ideas in the form of concentrated little shapes is not new; it has been around for millennia. It is to the ancient ideas expressed in the magical and esoteric world that we can best turn now, for suitable symbols to deepen our psychic insight.

Once again, superstition can stand in your way here if you let it. The traditional idea of the magician brings to mind all sorts of sinister and unspeakable markings, each with a supposedly dire and terrible intention. This superstitious picture is simply an obstruction, so make every effort to forget it. As with the Tarot, I am not suggesting that you practise magic or anything remotely like it. I simply recommend that you let your eye wander over some of the signs and signals of the older spiritual traditions. They are a language in themselves and have been formed out of the experience of many thousands of years. These symbols will have their subtle psychic effect, using their shape, and shape alone. Colour is not essential for them to touch a deep part of you. But on to the exercise:

1 *Let your eye wander over the following illustrations. They are selected from a vast range.*

2 *Each one would be best looked at on a page of its own, so if some catch your fancy, trace them out individually for yourself. Letting a symbol touch you enough to want to draw it by hand will produce a tremendous boost in your understanding of it.*

Many of these symbols you will recognize from astrology, if you have studied it. Don't make the mistake of thinking that because you recognize that a certain glyph means for example 'Saturn' that you know it. These symbols have a meaning that is more than just the word that goes with them. Have a look over these and see what you feel. Don't expect fireworks, or a sudden speech about your feelings to pop into your head. Just let your eye wander and see what comes up.

3 *Return to them from time to time, and hunt out some more if you feel so inclined.*

EXERCISE: Moving inwards

The first two exercises were designed to stimulate your imagination from the outside. From now on you will begin to work visually on

the inside. In other words, you have to actually imagine. The following exercise will help you to make the change from out to in. It is an immensely useful psychic developer, yet as with most good exercises, it is also very simple.

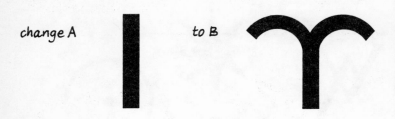

1 *Look at the two shapes in front of you.*

2 *Now cover up shape B, and look at shape A.*

3 *In your mind's eye, while looking at A, make it move in such a way that it transforms itself into B. Actually see the line dividing, and turning gracefully over at the ends. Most people see the two new arms that split out and curl over as moving out and round together at the same time and at the same speed.*

4 *Try it again as before, only this time see one arm going faster than the other.*

5 *Do it again and see one arm waiting until the other is complete before it moves. You will become aware that there is plenty of scope for variation even in this simple shape change.*

6 *Now try your imagination on the following slightly more complex designs.*

Visualization

This section marks something of a leap on the psychic path. Until now you have been dealing with lines and shapes that actually exist. They are there, out in front of you; written down and existing on paper for all to see. You now enter a new dimension. From here on you are going to be working completely in your own head with images that come from you alone. Only you will see these images, and in one sense, you are their creator. Although they may be images of things that are around you in the world, the versions that you create in your mind can take on whatever shape you give them. They are unique. They are in no way subject to the laws and rules of the physical world around you. A tree in your head could start as a tree and end up going absolutely anywhere! By observing the way the creations in this new inner world move and behave, you can begin to learn a lot about the laws and customs of the barely explored, non-physical kingdom of the Psyche.

The process of deliberately trying to see things in your mind's eye is called visualization.

EXERCISE: *Rotating the cross*

You will need to be in a quiet frame of mind and on your own to get the best out of visualization exercises. So take a few minutes to be by yourself in as tranquil a setting as you can. After your first time, you can try it anywhere you want.

1 *Close your eyes and imagine a cross. The sort of cross you would see on top of a church spire. Picture it made in whatever substance, texture and colour you wish.*

2 *Now, holding the image clearly in your mind, slowly rotate it until it is upside down. Continue to rotate it until it has gone round a full 360 degrees and is upright again.*

That's all there is to it. (I had better say that the cross symbol is by no means an exclusively Christian symbol. It dates back to Egyptian times and beyond. Certainly, no disrespect is intended by suggesting it be moved around in this way!)

A few people find this first attempt at deliberately making inner pictures to order, a little tricky. They say they can see absolutely nothing, but persevere and you *will* succeed. Anyone can do it, after a few minutes at the most.

When moving or rotating things, it is worth noting whether you feel happier about moving them left to right, or vice versa; clockwise or anti-clockwise. People have different instincts on this. For example, on the cross symbol exercise, when you started to rotate it, what point did it rotate around, and which way did it go? Did it revolve around the base, as if it was the hand of a clock going round. Or did it spin around on itself in one place, as if it were a wheel? Did it do something else? Notice all such details in your visualizations, especially about the way things move.

Always leave your visualization as you find it. This is important. If your symbol starts upright in your mind, wherever possible put it back that way after you've moved it. Leaving things at odd angles can leave you feeling a little odd yourself!

EXERCISE: *Seeing stars*

The five-pointed star is an ancient and very harmonious symbol, full of good associations and meaning. Use it as the basis for the following visualization.

1 *Picture in your mind a five-pointed star. It needn't look exactly like the drawing. That is just there to make sure you know roughly what shape I am talking about. Your star can be whatever colour and style you come up with. Gold, silver or blue are my favourites. Try to keep its actual proportions roughly the same as the illustration though.*

2 *Hold it in your mind.*

3 *When you can clearly see all five limbs of it . . . clothe it with flowers.*

4 *Hold your new image in your mind.*

5 *Now gently wobble it from side to side.*

6 *Return it to its upright position and let it dissolve. Don't forget this last step of tidying up, and putting things back as you found them.*

You will have to be in a fairly tranquil state of mind to do this exercise. So try it when you are in different moods, and see which mood is best.

This little visualization, contains a huge amount of potential, even though it doesn't seem to be much on paper. Don't be surprised if you can't get it first try. There is a lot to do here and you may be under-estimating what you are asking of yourself. If you find you can't quite get it all in your mind clearly at first, try it last thing before going to sleep for a couple of nights (no more). It will come in the end, of that you can be sure; and when it does, it often brings with it some pleasant feelings.

EXERCISE: *Walking into a picture*

There are many more such visualization techniques, some of them much more lengthy. One such, sometimes referred to as 'path-working' involves listening to another person as they guide you through a journey into your imagaination and back out again. You close your eyes, in a relazed and friendly environment and simply concentrate on seeing the imaginary journey unfolding before you in all its detail in your head. The vital factor in such 'path-workings' is the person who is telling the story. It is a beautiful thing to do once or twice if you know a sensitive and qualified person who can guide you through it. I'm afraid I can't recommend trying it from a book, or even from a tape, and certainly don't just get together with a friend and make one up.

Here, however, is something along the same lines. It will require you to set aside a little time and space (preferably, retreat to a quiet room for this) and to follow these instructions closely. It involves the use of a card from your Tarot pack. You will also need a candle.

1 *First scan through your pack, and find the card that inspires in you the greatest feeling of cheerfulness and positivity. (Optimism and lightheartedness are the best moods to bring on psychic development.)*

2 *Sit down somewhere comfortable and private, and preferably where the lighting is dim, propping the card up in front of you at about reading distance, illuminate it gently by candlelight, but don't put the candle so close that it catches your attention more than the card.*

3 *Sit quietly for a minute or two and let your glance fall on the card, from time to time.*

Don't stare at it; in fact, don't really try to do anything specific just yet. Simply sit as quietly and calmly as you can, noticing your card from time to time. You might like to listen to the sound of your own breath for a few seconds.

4 *Close your eyes and start the visualization. Picture your Tarot card growing larger and larger before you, until it is the size of a big screen.*

5 *You are now going to walk into the picture on this screen and see what you find. Climb over the edge of your card and into the picture. From here on you are on your own.*

6 *After you have done whatever small thing you do in your card (perhaps talking to whoever is in the picture, or looking behind or inside some object, or listening to any imaginary sounds, checking clothes, witnessing some event) you must always climb out of the card the way you went in.*

7 *Now shrink the card back to it's original size.*

8 *Physically, back in real life, pick up the card and slap it face down on to the table and forget it. The visualization is finished.*

9 *Stand up when you have opened your eyes, and go and do some utterly mundane and preferably physical action. Make a cup of tea, tidy up a room, clean the kitchen, even go to the loo!*

At moments like these, when you are returning to the everyday solid world, such earthbound activities will help your psychic growth and stability a lot. This steadying after the exercise phase, is as important as the exercise itself. That goes for all the other exercises in this book as well.

A word about memory
The images of your imagination do not store themselves in your day to day memory. They have to be created anew each time. This is one of their beautiful qualities. So if, in your imagination, you decide to go on a journey, you might find it hard to remember your imaginary way back. And if you do try to remember the sequence of your journey, for the purposes of retracing your steps, you will find your ability to visualize won't work!

So at this stage restrain yourself from epic visual wanderings over the horizon of your Tarot pictures. (You can always make what is over there come to you, if you are curious. Anything is possible remember.) Long inner voyages are best done accompanied by a guide who stays firmly in the physical world, and does all the remembering and thinking for you.

EXERCISE: Candle power

Here is another good way of developing a feeling for your inner world. This brief exercise is actually the tip of the iceberg in a huge mystery too great to go into in this book, and perhaps any book. So start small, and see if you are led in your daily life toward some other way of increasing your understanding of any secrets you may stumble on here.

Candle meditation is quite a specialized and well established practice. We shall use the basic technique of it to arouse our perceptions to go even further within . . . deeper than we have with any of the exercises so far.

1 Find yourself some time, a quiet, darkened room and a plain and simple candle. A straight white wax one in a saucer or simple candleholder will do nicely. You will also need something with which to snuff out your candle. The darker the room the better.

2 Sit in complete darkness for a few minutes, gently slowing down and settling, perhaps feeling your breathing coming and going. Have the candle, the snuffer, and some matches ready in front of you in about the same position as the card was in the last exercise . . . at a comfortable, easy reaching distance. Be calm.

3 Light the candle. Be as smooth and as efficient about it as you can. (Have a test run before the exercise proper, with the lights on to make sure the wick is all right, matches strike, snuffer snuffs, etc.)

4 Blow out the match and dispose of it safely.

5 Settle yourself again. As you do so, watch the flame of the candle carefully. Concentrate on it as it gently flickers, for about a minute, perhaps two. The exact time is not important.

6 *Now reach out and quietly snuff out the candle.*

7 *Close your eyes, and look at the image that is left on your retina.*
Focus on it, eliminating any other requests for your attention.
Let your attention rest here for as long as there is anything left to
look at.

8 *After five or ten minutes open your eyes, relight your candle,*
and prepare to re-enter the normal everyday world in whatever
way you feel is suitable. Get up and turn the lights on and, if
you can, let your candle burn for a while. Don't be in any hurry
to blow it out.

To comment too much on your likely experience in this exercise
would be to risk spoiling it for you. So simply try to be as calm as
possible when you do it, and watch for the pleasantly unexpected.
This exercise can only be done a few times and produce results, so
try to put as much into it at first as possible. As your psychic abilities
grow, you will outgrow it.

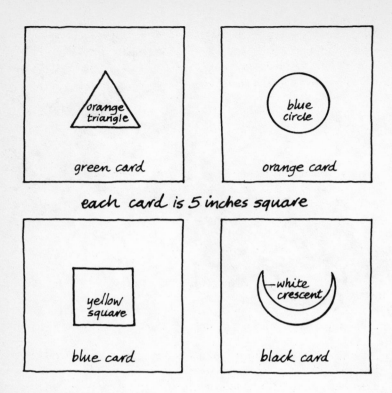

EXERCISE: *Visions*

This final exercise is the ultimate in imaginary experiences. It amounts to a deliberate hallucination in broad daylight with your eyes wide open! Rest assured, it is perfectly safe. Do it every day if you can. Because there is no colour in this book, you will first need to do some hand work. If you want to grow psychically the little work involved will be worthwhile. You need a set of four cards.

The best way of doing this is to buy coloured paper in simple primary tones and stick it on to card. Stick the background colour on first, then cut out and overlay the inner shape. For the circle and the crescent, draw around the bottom of a glass or other round object.

Stage One
Make yourself comfortable, in a quiet, private place.

1 *Set one of the squares in front of you, making sure plenty of light*

falls on it, preferably from a light source that is out of direct sight, behind you. Look at the card for about three minutes. Don't force anything, just keep your gaze gently on the card for as long as you can.

2 Now close your eyes, and you will see a faint, but perceptible likeness of the shape of the card in your inner vision. However, the colours will be completely different.

3 Watch your inner image placidly, making no attempt to change it in any way. It will come and go, fading and growing stronger of its own accord until it disappears altogether. Let it fade and open your eyes. Don't force anything.

4 Repeat the procedure with all four cards.

Stage Two

5 Repeat steps 1 to 4 on three or four days; they don't have to be consecutive days, but they should be fairly close together.

6 After about a week you will find you can see the cards clearly in living visual colour whenever you want, simply by closing your eyes and waiting. You won't first need to sit looking at the cards. That is the second stage.

Stage Three

The third stage requires a little more practice.

7 One day, when you are confident that you can see a shape nice and vividly inside . . . simply open your eyes. The image will not disappear, but will hang there, suspended in space before you. A vision.

It may take a little work first, but keep practising, and try for this effect. It will bring in its wake an unconscious increase of understanding, that will show itself as enhanced psychic sensitivity.

8 Be sure to give plenty of attention to the real world, after your hallucination image has faded beyond your perception. Get up and do something simple, and preferably non-psychic and physical.

This exercise works unconsciously and whether you like it or not produces an effect on your inner mind. It alters the way you think of yourself in relation to the world around you. The way to get the best out of it is to do it, but give it little or no thought. Simply get on with your life. All the rest will follow automatically.

4
AWAKEN TO
AN INNER WORLD

We are all very used to living in the physical world. If you have done the exercises in the last three chapters, you will be beginning to awaken to another inner world. I hope you are getting used to it. In this inner world, thoughts and feelings are as real as, say, tables and chairs are in the outer physical world. Small sensations, and subtle perceptions are the building blocks of our psychic dimension, and like the things of the physical world, they are put together according to certain patterns and are subject to certain rules. We are mere beginners, so don't be upset if you cannot say exactly what the rules are yet. That will come in time, and as I keep repeating, impatience is the one thing that repels psychic experience more than anything.

However, rules there are, just as in real life, and most of the basic ones are pretty easy to keep. 'Out here', whatever your abilities, you still have to breathe, eat, drive on the appropriate side of the road, send your children to school, and refrain from acts of mayhem etc., if you don't want to bring yourself into conflict with certain laws of living. These rules, as I said are not difficult to stick by and they are there mainly to keep us in harmony with the physical world we live in. Disobedience is unnatural and out of the question. Never for a second would we consider doing a totally random thing in the material world. A lot of very real damage could result from, say, using a gun in an unthinking, random way. Or, less spectacularly, leaving a large wooden wardrobe where it was not supposed to be! Well, by now if you have had any experiences as a result of doing the previous exercises, you should be ready to benefit from knowing one or two basic rules of the inner world. It will be enormously encouraging to your psychic development for the future. The rules of psychic growth concern your feelings and attitudes, rather than what you do.

Psychic ability enables you to cross the borders of your body and to become aware of things that are at a distance and completely separate from you both physically and in time. Put at it's most basic, it is psychically possible to be in bed in Newcastle, and yet to have a very real knowledge of something taking place in Trafalgar Square. Psychic development enables you to weaken the boundaries of where and when you exist and experience. As these boundaries fall away, your identity and ego begin to fall away, and become looser. This is natural and beneficial. Developing psychically actually weakens your ego. The sharp line between you, and what you think is not you, starts to become less distinct. In a way you become softer around the edges! It is important to realize this tendency. Our ego, which is basically who we think we are at any moment, is a very comfortable commodity for most of us. For better or worse, we feel at home with it. We recognize it as us, our self-image, you might say.

The ego barrier

At this stage in your development, you must begin to be aware of the fact that your ego is very much a tool of the material world. In the psychic world, it is too dense and soon becomes an obstacle. You will find that there, everything is working toward dispersing it, or trying to spread it out and refining it in some way, to make it very much less yours and yours alone.

This lessening of the importance of your own well-worn and familiar identity as a major means to psychic success can break through into your daily life. The results should be good. It will re-awaken in you a deeper feeling of sympathy, and well-being for the people around you and almost certainly bring a wish in you to deepen and change your attitude to yourself and your idea about your place in the universe. This is one of the 'eye-opening' side effects of seeking psychic growth that I mentioned earlier.

Psychics as a group are not selfish people. Every one that I have met, without exception, is motivated by a sense of wanting to do some good in the world. Even the most eccentric, flamboyant, and apparently ego-maniacal among them show a deep sense of righteousness and honesty when you get to know them even slightly. So here is one of the basic rules of the psychic world. You cannot progress in your psychic growth beyond a very elementary point, if you are doing it only for your own personal glory. The key word is only. None of us is perfect, and there will always be an element of self interest in whatever we do. But you must find that part of you that is interested in psychic growth for more than your own personal benefit, if you want to enrich your clairvoyant abilities. Ego as a motive simply won't work. If this last point confuses you, or you think you have to start being exceptionally nice, simply ignore what I've said. Carry on and do the exercises in the following chapters, and enjoy yourself. Your enjoyment will clear up any uncertainties. Seeking your own inner fulfilment, in harmony with the fulfilment of the world around you, is not an egocentric wish, so try to find some sympathy with this idea and you will progress in leaps and bounds.

Just as food is nourishment for your body, feelings are food for your psyche, and some foods are better and richer than others! A diet of competitiveness, boredom or frustration will not produce a well formed psychic sense. But there are some feelings that are extremely beneficial. So what is the best food for the budding psychic? The word I am about to re-introduce you to is one that has all but fallen out of everyday usage. The word is veneration (reverence). Believe it or not, the richest food to stimulate psychic growth is veneration. Although the physical world may be a bit scarce on things to inspire veneration at first sight, your own inner world is a rich source of it. Veneration, respect, wonder, adoration, all these are powerful and safe stimulants towards fantastic increases in psychic growth.

You may have to search long and hard to rediscover this feeling within yourself, so let me clarify further. First of all, why are we even looking for it? Why are we not just doing more psychic exercises? Cast your mind back to Chapter One. In it, I hope you developed an understanding of how simple mental ideas could be the triggers that started the ball rolling on far-reaching psychic processes that weren't mental themselves. Like the act of pulling a trigger, the apparently small move causes a huge event to happen. This is the process we are trying to do again here. By holding the idea of veneration in your mind every now and again, you will experience within yourself a psychic change of gear. Your perceptions and sensitivity of clairvoyance will step up enormously.

Of course, you will have to rediscover the meaning of veneration, and actually feel the feeling of it as best you can. Perhaps the following will help. Once again we go back to childhood for our first recollections of feelings in their purest form.

When you were a very small child, was there some person into whose company you went with a kind of awe? Not fear, mind you. Did you hesitate at the door of a room they were in, out of respect, hardly daring to turn the handle? Perhaps it was their office, or a

living room where you knew the grown ups were sitting. I must stress that it doesn't matter here whether the person in question actually deserved such veneration. What matters is, can you now recall the beginnings of that feeling that they inspired in you?

Adults feel awe and wonder at things in the natural world. Usually spectacular things, such as waterfalls, storms, mountains and sunsets. However, this is only part of the feeling of veneration. The modern adult removes the personal element when having feelings about nature, and it is exactly this personal element to which I am trying to redirect you. Have a mental search around your childhood and see if there was someone who played this part, even for a moment in your life. Note, again, there should be no tinge of fear in this feeling, only an intense respect and a natural humility on your part. Most people can find such a figure in their past, but do not realize the power of this short-lived feeling that arose in them. If you can find and somehow rekindle veneration again, you will begin to attract qualities from within yourself to which you can attach it, and a rich cycle of psychic growth can begin.

Later on you may find yourself feeling this veneration for natural things, such as trees, the sky, or a favourite river. At this stage of your psychic development however, simply look back into your childhood, and try to get a feel for it from your memory. You will recognize it then when it arises in you as a result of doing some of the exercises in the next chapter.

Be good!

There are many rules and laws that will help you in the psychic kingdom. The trouble with many of them is that when you actually say them or write them down they sound like rather pious, moral advice. The sort of thing a worthy old Victorian grandparent might recommend! For example:

As your psychic abilities begin to wake up, you have to be very careful to be of good character. Whereas you might have been scrupulously honest before, you might suddenly find yourself with the tendency to start lying! So if I advise you to be sure to watch your step and to resist the temptation to tell lies in your daily life, you might think that I was simply preaching a sermon on self-improvement. Actually; I'm not. I personally don't suffer the consequences of your honesty or lack of it, so it doesn't really affect me how you behave. But what I do know is this. There are very good reasons why a normal person's sense of what is honest or dishonest could easily be shaken temporarily as a result of opening themselves up to psychic growth. I also know this is a short-lived, minor teething trouble that need cause no concern, if a person is made aware of it. There are very good psycho-spiritual reasons for these changes in our character, and one need not take any blame for such lapses occurring.

Take the instance of lying. This arises from a combination of many new mental factors in your life. Firstly your enthusiasm will be roused to an unusual degree if you have success in some of the exercises. A new world seems to be opening up, and you want to tell about it. But when it comes to talking, you can't seem to find the thing you want to say in the place in your head where you are used to finding the things you usually talk about! As I said earlier, your imagination will not be stored in your usual abstract memory. In actual fact, your imagination stores in the same place as your feelings of want and desire. So when you do find the information that you are so keen on sharing, it brings with it a lot of unusual extra feelings from your desire department! The result is you may suddenly feel an urge to say anything, simply out of a strong desire to speak ... and all this before you've really realized what is happening to you.

It's not over yet either. Your poor ego which, meanwhile, was having a hard time existing at all on the inner planes, suddenly spots its chance, springs to life with a vengeance, and starts doing things to revive its former glory, to regain its monopoly on your experience. As you can see, a certain amount of confusion could enter into the picture. You could end up saying absolutely anything!

Add to this the increased sensitivity that your new found psychic abilities will bring you, and which will mean that you won't simply be able to turn your head away and pretend that you are not feeling any of this turbulence. You will have an urge to stop and work out what's going on. It's a situation where you had best be on your guard, observe your new tendencies, and try to be of good character! And that's where we came in. So do be as clear thinking, and sober as possible when you do these psychic exercises. There are very good reasons for cultivating all the traditional virtues if you want to experience the heights of psychic perception. There are also many potential little traps like the above one of lying or distortion of the truth.

However all these rather complicated matters are easily contained in the advice that I gave you earlier. While undergoing psychic development, be of as good moral character as you can. Try to be as stable as possible in your daily life. Sudden decisions of a far-reaching kind in your everyday life should be looked at with great caution.

All the above advice is based on experience and is given to help you achieve what, by reading this book, you obviously want to achieve. From now on there will be more of this broader advice mixed in with the exercises, as you should be beginning to show the first traces of your natural clairvoyance by now. Enjoy it — and your daily life too.

5
How to Use Your Psychic Awareness

From now on, try to work with the ideas of the last chapter firmly at the back of your mind. You needn't make any special effort or anything. All you need do is to feel some sympathy in yourself for the idea, and it will grow automatically without your worrying about it. It may encourage you to know that, in simpler times, a personal feeling of reverence and natural awe came easily. Things that were worthy of real honour and respect stood out very clearly from their surroundings. Today, however, uncertainty is a perfectly forgivable state of mind, considering the way we are evolving. Now, when we want to give expression to the natural emotion that there is something higher than our egos (at the last opinion poll conducted by Gallup, over seventy per cent of the population said they believed there was a god — whatever that was!) the only reliable place to look is into our own inner life of thought and feeling.

There are still obviously awe-inspiring things outside and around us. Who could not be impressed when they stand outside on a clear night and look up at the stars? But as I have said, the feelings that this brings tend to leave us feeling a little insignificant and depersonalized. We can easily just walk away from the experience feeling slightly stunned, shrugging our shoulders with a 'what on earth had all that got to do with me?' sort or feeling. What will help us most for psychic growth now will be the more personal, heartfelt feeling from inside ourselves.

Bearing all this in mind we are now going to do some concentration exercises.

Remember how, in Chapter Three, we deliberately looked at the Tarot and various other symbols in order to enhance our inner senses? Hopefully, the images have given rise in you to a few new sensations and emotions at least. They may be mysterious and unresolved as yet, but that doesn't matter. The images caused feelings in you, thanks to your concentration on them.

Well now, instead of looking at man/woman-made symbols we are going to look, in the same sort of imaginative way, at the natural world around us. In the following exercises the 'god created' world of nature is going to be the starting point for our attention and through it, by a similar process to that of before, we will contact psychic forces flowing in us at an even deeper level. The whole world of nature around us (*not* the man-made world, please note) is to be seen as one giant symbol or Tarot card, with a message on it to arouse in us psychic forces hidden deep.

Hopefully not too deep however, and certainly pleasant I can assure you.

Concentration

From now on, even when we are not consciously doing a specific exercise, we must try to slow down the tendency to let our attention dart from one thing to another, then back again and so on. You will never be able to concentrate perfectly for a long time on one thing, so don't try (psychically sensitive concentration must be nurtured indirectly). The idea now for our purposes is to be aware that you have this overwhelming tendency to refocus your attention at high speed from one thing to another. Concentration always darts excitely from point to point, both inside you and outside you. Being aware that you do this is all you need, in order to control the process to a large degree.

From now on, merely make a mental acknowledgement of the possibility of slowing it down a little. If you find yourself looking at, say, a tree let your attention dwell there. If you look up, let your eyes linger with the sky for just that little bit longer (bearing in mind, common sense and safety etc.). The first five or six times, you may have to consciously will yourself not to be distracted too soon. Your ability will improve at least a hundred per cent quite soon, largely as a result of the flitting-about habit being pointed out to you and your unconscious mind slowly harmonizing itself with the idea of helping you to slow it down.

The reason we are making an effort to use our concentration is in order to channel ourselves into a rich supply of psychic energy, and we need concentration to hold us firmly in contact for long enough to let the energy get through. The feelings that the following exercises will inspire will be the building blocks out of which you will be creating and restoring to use certain undernourished psychic centres in the body. In actual fact, the necessary food for these psychic sense organs has always been around us, but we have been a little too quick to disconnect from the supply of it. Now you are simply putting your senses on to the right things, concentrating for a little longer, and letting the feelings build. What particular psychic organ gets built; how, when and where it is in your body, does not matter at this stage. This is a natural process that looks after itself automatically. More about that later. Please don't make your concentrating into, 'I have got to stare at this and extract the maximum from it' sort of activity. At the first hint of tension, stop, rest, and give no thought to psychic growth for at least a day, or as long as you like.

EXERCISE: Growth and decay

This exercise, and those that follow it, is one that you do over a day or two at first, and then as much and whenever you want. Simply give your attention to things and events in nature that are in the process of growing, flourishing, strengthening in some way. And also, equally, to natural things and events that are decaying, dying, fading or withering.

1 *First decide in your mind what these things and events are.*

There are many of them, even for confirmed city dwellers, and they will pop easily to mind in due course. But here are a few guidelines. You could focus on things such as:

A blossoming bough on a tree.
Flowers growing in a window box.
A young puppy or colt.
Trees in winter.
Dead grass.
An ageing dog or bird.

Things tend to strike you in your daily life after a day or so of digesting this growing/decaying idea, so no hurry. It happens rather in this way:

You're on your way to the shops when suddenly you see something, and the thought pops into your head, 'That's a growing sort of thing!' or 'Hmm, that looks a bit withered!' . . . and you are away at once in your imagination, looking at it and noticing it.

Remember, flourishing, blossoming, growing and fading, decaying, wilting. These are the two forces to tune in to.

2 *After a while of turning your attention to things that are obviously growing and things that are obviously withering you will begin to notice specific feelings. arising in yourself.*

This is an important stage. Grasp these feelings. You will find that, no matter which of millions of possible decaying objects you look at, from a dead bird to a huge old oak, there will arise in you only the one distinct feeling. Similarly, the myriad range of growing and blossoming things will all produce within you but one feeling . . . a different one, of course. You will find two distinct feelings associated with, on the one hand expanding and flourishing, and on the other fading and decaying.

By concentrating on growing, a feeling rather like a sunrise will happen.

By concentrating on decaying, you will feel a sensation like the moon slowly rising on the horizon.

Hold on to these two forces as they arise in you; fix your attention on the feelings as intently as you can, surrender to these sensations. These are your first perceptions of a psychic reality and to begin with they are very dim and elusive.

3 *This is the easy bit. Simply continue to focus as in Step Two, and suddenly an amazing thing will happen. (It could take a little while, depending on the individual.)*

Your soul will feel as if it is swelling outwards, and instead of having a mere feeling within you, you will get the distinct awareness that you are standing before a definite energy force that makes itself felt to you. More than a feeling now, and it has its own independent existence. The magic thing is you can not actually see it as such, yet you know it is there.

All this happens quite naturally as a result of simply alternating your attention on growth or decay in nature, in a patient and open way.

Inevitably, you will have great difficulty explaining to anyone who has not done this exercise that you are not going mad! So keep your perceptions to yourself for now. The presence of the energy that you feel is as real as anything in the material world, you are merely perceiving something that is non-physical. You will get to know these forces very well as time goes by. Indeed, you may know them already. Many people have a great natural clairvoyant sense, that is easily awoken, and the above exercise may be all that is needed to free in them a very developed natural sensitivity. If that isn't you, simply do the exercise and wait patiently. Soon enough the two forces will make themselves known to you in a real and tangible inner way.

The beginnings of psychic vision

Unlike the simple, earlier exercises, this one may have to be read through once or twice, to absorb the idea. Believe me, I'm trying to make it as straightforward as possible.

In the last exercise we discovered through deliberate and keen observation, the existence of two forces of energy: one associated with growing, and one with withering or fading. Although at first we needed our imagination to open ourselves up to perceiving them, we eventually became aware of them in a very real way (a psychic way), and they now have an existence of their own. Looking back, you may not quite be able to remember just how real they were, but next time you choose to concentrate, you will realize that they are still there. This is one of the quirks of the early stages of psychic memory.

In this new exercise we are going to learn ways of knowing more of these forces. We are going to see them in a psychic way. The vision that results from this exercise filters through over a period of time until it eventually becomes one of your daily senses.

EXERCISE: *Lines and shapes*

In the material world, growth and decay have associated with them definite lines and shapes. All material things that are under the influence of the growth force tend to show one particular style of lines and shapes. Similarly, all the events and objects influenced by the fading force will show another distinct type of line and shape. I am not talking here about colour. It is only lines and shapes that will make themselves felt at the moment.

1 *Begin to look for very specific lines, shapes and forms, that surround the two forces.*

They are not random or arbitrary. A growing force always arranges things in growth type lines, and a decaying one in decay type lines. You must tune in to the feelings of each and let your psychic vision grow. This is a completely new way of looking, so expect a few days' experiment at least. What you are trying to do is connect the feelings of the forces you have discovered with the actual shapes that always surround them.

2 *You probably expect me to indicate what the particular lines and shapes are. I am not going to do so. If you are aware of the two forces and have done even a few of the previous exercises, you will be able to psychically see for yourself!*

Anyway, there are many variations on the two basic visual themes of growing and decaying, so you will have plenty of opportunity of coming to your own conclusions in your own time!

By doing this exercise you will begin to feel a new way of seeing into a thing, rather than simply letting your eyes rest on it. You will perceive some of its essence. There is a slight knack to it, but you will get it eventually. It is almost as if you have to ignore the thing you are looking at, first glance, until you get the perception of its feeling (growth or decay). Then you concentrate on the object for a second and see what you notice. Repeat this concentration, inside and outside, until a definite awareness of lines of force, and patterns of form, condenses in your mind. It may sound complicated, but it is perfectly natural.

After a while, when you are familiar with the feelings of growth and decay, you will be ready to try the following:

Tune in to one or other force. Simply search around in yourself until you find it for a split second. You won't need to have anything in front of you to inspire it any more. Then, without closing your eyes, try to see in the air in front of you the kind of forms this feeling would take, if it could suddenly show itself visually.

From now on, growth and decay will no longer be mere dry words for you. Let them be actual entities, that evoke in your inner mind actual forms. This is the beginning of a new psychic way of seeing.

Psychic hearing

The ear is capable of conveying feelings even more powerfully, in some ways, than the eye. The mystical power of music shows just what a pathway hearing is into our hidden psychic side, but you will need sharp listening powers of attention in the following exercises.

When you listen to the sounds of the world around you, discriminate between sounds that are produced by inanimate or lifeless things, and sounds that come from living creatures (actual sounds only, please; not from radio, tape, compact-disc, TV, stereo, or any of the other popular sound sources, for these exercises).

Lifeless sounds, for example, would be a siren, a bell or something falling. Living sounds would be those from the animal kingdom, including humans. Make a point of discriminating between the two types of sound in your daily life. Then, when you've done this for a while, proceed to the next stage.

Begin to notice that, with lifeless sound, say, when a bell is rung, we hear the sound and connect a feeling with it (either more or less pleasant). The sound causes a simple effect in us. No more.

But when you hear a sound emitted by a living thing, there is another feeling . . . an extra dimension. This second feeling is the inward experience of the creature making the sound. This second component, found only in living sound, is the key to great psychic insight. Notice it with all your inner sensitivity. Concentrate on the fact that the sound that is coming to you is telling you of something that lies completely outside your being. It is the expression of another soul.

Now try to bridge the gap, unite yourself completely with the pleasure, pain or whatever other feeling that the sound is conveying.

It doesn't matter whether you like or dislike the sound (that is only your reaction to lifeless sound). Go beyond this. Try to fill yourself inwardly with every bit of the feeling being experienced by the being that made the noise.

By doing this whenever you can, you bring yourself into sympathy with the hidden essence of the alive sounds that reach your ears. A new kind of hearing is implanted in you. You develop the psychic ability to merge with the being that produced the sound. Great insight comes with success at this, and you may surprise yourself with what you can achieve.

This new faculty for being sensitive to sound can spread quickly throughout your whole life. It is as if you are hearing directly with your emotions and thoughts, rather than just with your ears. Natural sounds, animate or inanimate can begin to affect you much more deeply. Once this sort of hearing is awoken, all sound becomes a source of considerable information about the feelings and motives of whatever or who ever makes it. Things begin to 'speak' to you through noise and sound, whereas before only words could speak.

A large proportion of the living sounds that reach our ears are made by our fellow humans. Later on I will be going into more detail about how to get the best for our own psychic growth through the art of really listening to our brothers and sisters.

EXERCISE: *Colour cues*

After the previous long term and rather abstract exercises, here is something very simple and down-to-earth.

1 *From an art shop or a stationers buy several pieces of coloured card, as large as you can afford. The bigger the better. Get a red one, a blue one, a yellow one, and a green one, plus any other colour that catches your fancy. Pink and grey are suitable if you can't make up your mind.*

2 *In a good light, select one card and simply hold this card of your choice up in close in front of your face, so that you can see nothing but the colour on the card. Your first impression will probably be that of the smell of the new card. But after that, try to concentrate as follows!*

3 *Open yourself to the feelings evoked in you by the unbroken expanse of colour before you. Let your eyes go out of focus, and soak up the sea of tone. Look for tiny floating feelings in yourself that seem to fit with the colour.*

Can you feel the red in any particular part of your body?

What is the feeling or feelings connected with green?

Of the colours you chose for yourself, what feeling do they give you that you like?

If you can afford to do so, buy several shades of a colour, and see what it is about the shade you prefer that isn't in any of your feelings for the other shades. Get to know the feelings *within* you that are evoked by colours *outside* you. The size of the card will help your concentration, and so will your patience and ability to sit quietly and relaxed as you do this. It may feel a little silly, to be staring at a piece of coloured card like a short-sighted person reading a newspaper but, believe me, there are some definite differences in the feelings that the colours arouse in you. Learning which colour makes you feel what, will come in handy later on, when we start to develop our ability to see psychic colours.

Colour techniques

If you get discouraged by an inability to concentrate, try one or both of these techniques.

Have the card in front of you down on your knee. Sit and relax, centre yourself, and listen to your breath, in and out. Close your eyes calmly. Raise the card in front of you. Open your eyes and absorb the colour. Close your eyes again and look for feelings, gently and patiently. Repeat slowly, but stop before you get bored.

The glance method. Simply hold the card to one side and glance at it quickly every few seconds. Then close your eyes and hold the colour in your imagination. Repeat at speed, and then stop and contemplate.

Of course you may be one of the many people who can grasp their feelings for colour almost instantly without elaborate techniques. If so, that's fine, but do be sure you have a definite feeling within you for each tone, and are not just repeating what you might have read in an article or book on, say, painting or decorating.

Observing natural objects for psychic growth

The following exercise is of a more reflective kind and so has a slightly looser form than those suggested so far. The object is for you to do something that will enable you to discover in yourself certain new nuances of feeling. I am going to suggest an extremely simple activity, and some ideas to mull over in your mind as you carry this out. This is a subtle but very effective learning technique.

After a while, out of the two things given to you − the activity and the line of thought − a third thing arises in you which is your very own. A definite, personal, psychic insight seeps into your conscious mind.

As with all aspects of psychic growth, the following rule is true. Understanding gained by force and impatience will fade away and leave you, but insights that arise gradually, even over a short period of time, will stay yours for ever. I'm sure you know the feeling of rushing to tell someone about an amazing insight that you read only yesterday which is 'oh so true' . . . only to discover halfway through your conversation, that you can't seem to remember what you wanted to say!

EXERCISE: Mineral, Animal, Vegetable

Now, you are going to focus your observation on three things from the world of nature: a crystal, an animal and a plant. Start with the crystal and the animal.

1 *Find a crystal, preferably a beautiful one, but any sort will do. You may be able to borrow one, its size is not important, as long as it is an easy to look at lump of beautiful mineral matter.*

2 *Position yourself where you can observe an animal. This sounds a bit odd, I know, but it is necessary for this exercise, as follows: concentrate your attention on comparing the crystal with the animal.*

Put the crystal down where you can see it (not in your hand) and look. As you do this, let the following thoughts pass through your mind. Give as much of yourself as you can to these thoughts, and try not to let your mind wander. When it does, bring it back gently and think again.

'This crystal has a form of its own. That animal also has its own form. The crystal doesn't move; it remains fixed in its place. The animal changes its place all the time. It is the force of desire that causes it to change place. It changes its place because it *wants* to. The whole shape and form of the animal expresses the "wanting" force within it. Every part of it is in perfect harmony with the desire force that moves it. The stone, on the other hand, shows no trace of desire in its form. It is made up of forces that do not include desire.'

The action of observing, and the suggested line of thought, will produce results along the following lines:

Two quite distinct sensations will arise in you as a result of looking at a crystal, and looking at a living creature. Two clearly different auras, flavours, atmospheres, psychic impressions, call it what you will, will be perceived by you in connection with the differing forms.

Repeat this exercise regularly over a period of time and you will know very clearly what these psychic sensations are.

At first you will only get a glimmer of them when you actually have the objects in front of you, but with a little practice you will find that they grow into a feeling that stays with you and you will be able to summon them at will. It is from out of these feelings that forces arise in you that will build and strengthen your slumbering psychic sense organs, in particular your sense of psychic sight.

In connection with the above exercise I would ask the following:

Does the stone seem to have about it a blueish quality?

Does it generate in you a feeling like the one you experienced when you looked at the colour blue?

Perhaps it actually seems to glow blue, or blue-red for a moment when you look at it?

Did the animal seem to have a yellow-red colour connected with it?

Did it affect you with a yellow-red feel?

And what about plants? Where do they fit in? The feeling associated with any plant you choose to look at will be found to lie somehow between the feeling from the stone and the feeling of the animal. It is best described as a bit more than one and a bit less than the other! Nevertheless, it has its own distinct aura, just as do the rock and the animal. The best way to arrive at the plant feeling is to become quite sure of the animal and mineral feelings first. When you do receive a clear-cut plant impression, it will probably carry with it a greeny-pink quality.

The above exercise will eventually bring results, so don't give up after the first or second attempt. It is a powerful exercise and something of a conversation stopper! If you try to discuss your results with someone who isn't trying to develop in the same way, you will probably end up with all sorts of crossed lines. Humans are made up of body, mind and spirit, and most people are only practically interested in the things that have to do with body. If you start talking about your spiritual discoveries and adventures, people will simply have no idea what you are on about. A psychic exercise such as this has no meaning at all to a person who isn't doing it. If you talk to such a person about it, you will end up with the distinct impression that they are listening to you comprehending nothing, as if you were speaking in a different language!

EXERCISE: *Plant gazing*

Bearing in mind that objects in front of you inspire thoughts, and from these thoughts, feelings and sensations are developed, try the following exercise, which is probably better described as 'a meditation'. It also involves some visualization. Much of the

benefit from it will come from taking to heart the ideas that go with it. The practical side is really only looking hard and opening yourself up to certain impressions. You have to do both, to develop clear psychic vision. Your observation of what you choose to focus on will have to be at its keenest, and you will also need your imagination.

We are going to look at a plant, so you will need some time, quiet and privacy, and the plant of your choice. It is essential that on the first occasion, you do this exercise in calm conditions, but after that you are at liberty to do this or any other exercise whenever you have an opportunity in your daily life. Do go through it carefully first, to get clear in your head what it is you are trying to do and feel.

1 *Place in front of you a seed and observe it closely. Notice the shape, colour, texture and any other tiny peculiarities.*

2 *Let the following thought fill your mind:*

'From out of this tiny seed, a large and complex form will come into being.'

3 *Now picture in your imagination the plant that will grow:*

'What I am picturing in my mind will be brought out of this tiny seed as a result of the influence of light and earth. If what I see before me was only a replica of a seed, identical in every way in colour and shape, no amount of earth and light could produce from it a plant. All that will come from this seed is already compressed and concealed within it. There would be no such force in an imitation seed. This real seed I see before me contains something that is totally invisible to my eye. But later this force will become visible. With my powers of thought I can become aware of this force before it actually becomes visible.'

4 *Give this idea time to sink in deeply. Well beyond the point*
  where you would first think it would come to rest in your mind.

As a result, a feeling will make itself felt. The grain of seed will from time to time appear to be surrounded by a tiny luminous cloud. The colour feeling of this cloud will be bluish-lilac. Please note, it is not staring hard at the seed that will produce this effect. Your understanding and sensitivity to the ideas given above is what will make this force visible to your psychic eyes.

This is probably the hardest exercise in this book, so do it whenever you can, and don't get discouraged. Whether you actually get the above sensation or not is unimportant. The mere attempt will bring successful growth in many hidden ways, and your development will continue regardless of the outcome of this one exercise.

EXERCISE: Seeing the life force

The following, and final exercise in this chapter, is another way of getting an appreciation of the same force, but approaches the matter from a different direction.

1 *Place before you a fully mature plant, at the peak of its growth.*
  Let the following idea fill your mind:

'There is going to come a time when this plant will wither and die. There will be nothing left of what I see before me. My mind tells me that this plant produces seeds that will develop into new plants. Something that I cannot see tells me that this plant has in it a force that protects it from disappearing. I know that this force is there, but I can't actually see it, any more than I could physically see the force that was going to bring the plant into existence in the seed. There is something in the plant which is very real, but is invisible. I would like to see it.'

2 *If you are patient, a form rather like a flame will appear to surround the plant. It will be greenish-blue in the middle, perhaps with a slight red-yellow tinge around the edge.*

In exercises such as these, a world of beautiful colour awaits discovery. The tones of the psychic world are subtler but at the same time richer in feeling. Take your time and see what you can see.

6
THE HUMAN BODY:
A PSYCHIC VIEW

Each of the natural things you see around you has within it a force or energy. Colours, animals, minerals, sky, fire, even vegetables all give out their own particular message to anyone who cares to develop psychic sensitivity. Noticing these forces puts you in touch with a whole new dimension, lying as if behind and beyond the physical thing that your eyes rest upon. When you start to connect with the deeper dimension, an exciting stage of rapid growth begins for you. So much new information floods in about the psychic forces in the world around you, that you can get quite intoxicated ... even to the point where you sometimes have to close down your sensitivity for days at a time in order to digest what you are learning. You need to return and get yourself back into the routines and comfort of the good old mundane physical world!

A word now about Guardian Angels. It soon becomes obvious to anybody who has made the slightest progress in this clairvoyant way of appreciating things, that what is unfolding for them is not entirely happening as a direct result of their own will. When you strive to educate yourself psychically, a lot of so-called coincidences start happening. It is good to see such things for what they are and to benefit wherever possible.

Take, for example, the business of closing down your sensitivity for a few days to digest and reflect on a sudden burst of new insight. You do not suddenly, consciously decide 'I think that's enough for the moment. I now judge it to be a good thing to do no psychic development for four-and-a-half days. I'll start again next Thursday morning at half past nine.' Not at all. What is more likely to happen is this: you will be feeling very happy with your growth and new experiences, and looking forward to yet more awareness when, suddenly, the central heating breaks down, or your aged Aunt Maud rings up and asks to pay a visit for a few days. Or perhaps one of the children will be off school, or work will suddenly hot up beyond expectations. The first thing you will have to abandon will be your psychic growth!

Probably, in spite of your intentions, you will be so involved in whatever arises, you won't be able to get back into your cosy feeling of steady progress. Instead you will be forced to go along with whatever situation is unfolding. This slotting of your growth into your daily life is significant. The pattern of your clairvoyant growth, and indeed your life itself is not arbitrary. Often, after a short time has passed and you have gained a little perspective you will see that if you had managed to achieve what you set out to do (in this case, continue your psychic growth and satisfaction), you could well have ended up worse off in some way.

Psychic development makes situations like these so apparent that you can't help but conclude that some force other than your personal will is at work, arranging the pattern of your growth and indeed your very life for you! A word of warning though. All the above can only be noticed with the benefit of hindsight. You can't expect your guardian angel to arrange your life in any special way that you want, simply because you're beginning to notice his/her influence. You have to go ahead and live as if there were no such thing as a guardian angel. Indeed, as far as most people consider, there isn't. But more about spirits and angels later. For now, let's get back down to earth and look closely at us humans and, in particular, at that wonder of creation — the human body.

Become body aware

The human body is one huge psychic phenomenon. You need look no further than your own body, for an endless source of clairvoyant understanding. In general, though, until our bodies go wrong, we tend not to notice them. Only when ill do we really become body aware, and then we usually abdicate responsibility, turning to people who we regard as better qualified to know about bodies than ourselves.

The human body has come to be regarded as a realm for experts, doctors, biologists, surgeons, and other highly qualified practitioners. Without a knowledge of specialized research techniques we tend to assume that we can know very little about the body so we don't bother.

It is *not* my intention for one second to belittle the marvellous and beneficial mass of organized understanding of medical science. To

do so would make me very foolish. But what I would like to point out to anyone who wants to advance in their psychic sensitivity is this. The human body is not the domain of doctors and experts. It is the property of, and a gift to, you — or the individual who inhabits the body in question. You and me. We are in charge. We are all at liberty to explore our own body, to sense it for ourselves, how and where we want. There are mysteries and wonders in a human frame that no medical expert is any more qualified to experience than you or I, and it is to this magical side of the human body that, as growing psychics, we have to begin to become sensitive.

The popular view of the body that we have inherited is limiting. It suggests that the brain is really just an advanced computer; the heart is a kind of a pump; the nerves are a glorified electrical system, and the lungs are bellows. The eye is a kind of camera complete with film (retina), the ear demonstrates the theory of microphones, while the stomach and abdomen, that powerhouse of our first psychic experiences, is a kind of internal chemical factory, which only surgeons, or those who understand the mysteries of 'enzymes' and 'metabolic processes' can dare to approach! The body is thus reduced to the level of a machine, a series of complex systems that require a lot of thinking about. There is really no wonder then, that the psychic qualities of our bodies are never really noticed.

To our psychic perception, the human body is a softer experience, one we can begin to feel from within. Most people will admit, however half-heartedly, that a human body is not totally a physical

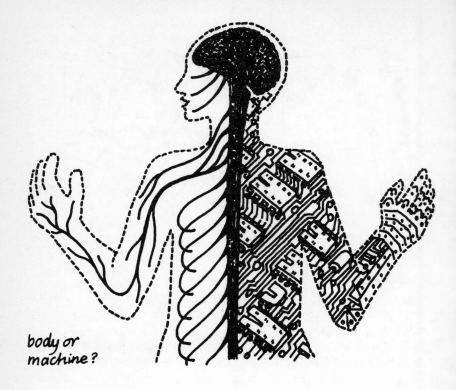

body or
machine?

phenomenon. Rather grudgingly, even the most materialistic person concedes the possibility that although it is a kind of machine, the human body may possess a vague, unidentifiable soul-force. That is as far as most people dare go in the face of all the scientific information available. It is not far enough.

A key idea
The popular scientific view says: 'The body is solid and real, and in it, supported by it, is a mysterious and rather abstract soul-force.' This is quite untrue. Psychic perception shows the complete opposite. The body exists ... yes, hard and solid, but it is the so-called 'mysterious and abstract soul force' that is creating the body and is in fact causing it to exist. Not the other way round. It is our psychic force that holds the body together, not the body that contains some lesser abstract force. The presence of spiritual energy is as important to the form of every organ in the body, rather as jelly mould is to the form of a jelly!

Try to accept this new perspective on your body as at least a possibility. You know from our experiences in the previous chapter that definite unseen psychic forces exist . . . you will have perceived them. So the above notion should be a little more than an abstract possibility to you by now. I might just add that you should probably feel some resistance to the above idea at first. If you are going to advance psychically, this is a good sign. If you don't experience any resistance, and you just shrug off this idea, the chances are you have only understood what I have said with the intellectual part of your mind. Try to take it a little more to heart. Probably also, your memory will argue that the forces you have felt so far were really rather subtle, and it may take a certain stretch of the imagination to see how such a fleeting psychic phenomenon could be strong enough to create and maintain such a heavy physical thing as a body . . . but these are early days, and our perceptions are young. Right now it is important to start to look at things the wrong way round as it were! To reflect on the possibility that our bodies are made up, first and foremost of psychic energy, which is then clothed in physical matter. It is the spirit of this energy that supports the physical body, and not the hard fleshy body that supports the spirit. Think about it.

What we will set about doing now is to turn our sensitivity in on ourselves and see what forces we can find at work in our bodies.

How to look at bodies

Try this way of looking at the human exterior for a while. Don't think of the body as a complex medical system for one second longer. Think of it, and actually try to see it, in separate sections, each one expressing a different quality, and with its own particular form. I will tell you what these sections are soon.

Now an important factor. You must consider each bit as if it were an entirely independent being. If you did the experiments with the Tarot pack you will probably remember an image on one card of lots of separate parts of the body, heads, hands and feet etc. This separating of the body is a very relevant psychic process. So try not to be squeamish about it! It is also very hard to describe without sounding nutty, so bear with me!

The head
Let's look at the head in a new way. Humans are set apart from the

animal kingdom by the fact that they walk upright. We don't start off this way. We begin as babies lying down, with our head level with the rest of our body. But from day one our heads do all they can to work their way upwards to the highest possible point. Unfortunately, they don't stop when they get there, they want to keep right on climbing! If you think that I'm being a little anti-head here, this is deliberate on my part. The head has had too much attention by far in our lives to date, so a bit of bad publicity for a change won't do it any harm.

The head creature (remember, that's how we're looking at it) imagines it's the king of the castle. However, in one sense it does absolutely nothing. Carrying it around, the body almost breaks its neck to protect the head from any sudden movement. The limbs reach out to get the head what it wants; the lungs and heart pump day and night to keep it supplied, and the stomach processes and churns vigorously to keep it happy. You'd think it was by far the most important part of the body. But there is a kind of deadness about the head. It doesn't really participate in the physical world at all. It just sits on top, receiving signals from all those busily working other parts.

Heads are heavy, round or oval, bony domes, concealing vulnerable, but equally dense innards. They are enclosing and hard, and usually covered in hair, and the only major contribution they make of their own is to ache! Take away the sensory equipment, and the head has little sensation.

Heads are very good at making impressions. They will try to show you what they want to show you, and they see what is most easily seen. Heads are very good at taking all the credit, too. They give no hint of where they get their information from. You could be forgiven for thinking that they are the actual suppliers. But they are not. In fact, they are simply 'middle men' who collect material from the outside world, and give it out in a different form. They have very little of their own to offer ... except of course, the headache. Heads are very poor bosses, and should not be listened to when they start to take control of the body.

Buried deep within a thick protective helmet of bone is the brain, the most inert part of the entire body. All its activity is silent and invisible. It scarcely moves. What goes on in it is anyone's guess. Certainly, medical science has no definite ideas, except to say that we use only a fraction of the brain's potential. This thought often gets researchers quite excited. They imagine all that other potential up there in the head, waiting to be discovered. Psychic observation shows that there are other ways of viewing this fact, and even the

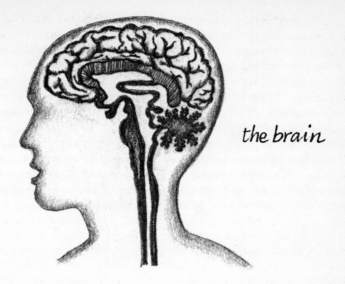

the brain

scientific world is coming round to this possibility. The psychic thinks of the brain as not so much an active 'doing' thing, but more as a kind of filter; an enormous resistor, designed to screen out huge amounts of information to enable us to live at the limited physical level we are designed to experience in the material world. Looked at like that, it is easy to see that the apparently unused potential is already fully at work, keeping some unknown reality at bay, and enabling us to function in an existence that might otherwise totally overwhelm us!

We feel most alive up in our head, but in fact, our feeling of aliveness does not come from our head. It is the first place we go to when we are conscious. We scratch it when we think, and knock other people's when we get angry! The first impressions on anything arise here, and if we think and worry too long, here is where they stay, giving us the feeling that we live in our head. Eventually, many of us start to believe we actually *are* our heads, and the body is nothing but a vehicle for carrying it around. Like a driver in a car. The head is the main event, sticking out above the clothed body and dealing with all the other heads around, as they pass, carried on their own bodies. So though the head does a lot of good things, psychically speaking, it can be a bit of an obstacle. Viewed as a being in itself the head is an utterly helpless creature. Just because it is the centre of the nervous system it seems to have delusions of grandeur and forgets its place in the harmony of the whole body.

I will not give you any exercises to encourage you to become aware of the feeling of your head, as so much of the modern, man-made world around us is very little more than one huge attempt to re-focus your energies onto this region. Reading, counting, talking, decision-making, artistry, even sex, have all been usurped by this power hungry organ. All this is much easier to see in other people, so try these head watching exercises and see what you can pick up with your psychic antennae.

Remember, though, no criticism must creep into your head while you watch other people's! As in all observing exercises, a deep respect for the souls whose bodies you are looking at should arise. If it doesn't, abandon the exercise until you feel more able to love those who you are looking at and learning from.

EXERCISE: Head watching

Next time you are in a group of people in a room, simply be aware of all the heads and the heads alone. Relegate the body to the same importance as the chair that the person is sitting on, or the wall or furniture nearby.

After a while, you will start to notice the different movements of heads. The heads of some people seem to float in space, with their bodies almost dangling off them. Other people's heads move and bounce around completely at the mercy of the body underneath them. Some sag forward as if ashamed or sleepy, while others are thrown back and seem to challenge the world around. Some move to the left when their owners speak, while others are drawn irresistibly to the right. Don't get drawn to studying faces alone; look at the whole head and how it moves.

EXERCISE: Moving experiences

Every head has a different feeling associated with it. The best way to get the feeling from it is to imitate the person's head movements and position with your own head. You can do this quite unobtrusively.

By moving your own head in the way that you see someone else's move you will generate inside yourself a tiny feeling of the emotions and forces that are operating on them. If necessary, repeat one position or gesture over and over, until you get a clear feeling inside of what the movement you are doing is saying to you.

Remember what I said about the head only being a middle man. Heads are really telling you about the situation in a lot of other places, too.

Making the movements of another person's head can bring on feelings in other parts of *your* body. A certain head gesture could, for example, make your stomach tighten, or perhaps give you a warm feeling around your own heart. You will be learning more about this later.

EXERCISE: *Imagination*

There is an ancient occult theory that the head that you have in this lifetime is created out of the forces that made your body in your previous lifetime. Whether you believe this or not doesn't matter, but it does give rise to the following exercise.

1 *Look at a head and imagine it as a body. The forehead is the chest, the lips and jaw are the lower trunk and legs, the cheeks and nose are the chest and stomach. The eyes and brow are the shoulders. Perhaps the ears are the arms.*

The exact correspondence between facial features and bodily organs is not one hundred per cent important. It will vary from face to face, so be flexible, though try to be specific in each case.

2 *What sort of a body do you see as a result of looking in this way at a person's head?*

Quite often, a very clear picture of a certain human frame can pop into your imagination. More likely though, is that you will have to build up the picture feature by feature. You may find it more suitable to picture a male body from a female head, and vice versa, as it is alleged that we change sex at each re-incarnation.

EXERCISE: *Clairvoyance 1*

It is quite common, when you have done the exercises recommended for a few weeks or months, for the following to occur.

You will be looking at someone's head when, suddenly, it will change into a quite different head; an entirely different face may appear. If this happens, avoid trying to conjure up explanations, or believing that you have seen a ghost or some such fantasy. You can regard this as a sign that you are becoming sensitized. You can even try to bring this phenomenon on deliberately, once you know it is possible. Use this glancing technique.

1 *Look at the head, and then look away almost as quickly.*

2 *Now look back and see if any of the features change. Continue this glancing for as long as it feels spontaneous.*

The idea is to look at the head as indirectly as possible, almost as if you really didn't want to see it. Your imagination will play a large part in this, and so will the lighting in the room as it falls on the head, but try to catch even the tiniest impression of a change if you see one.

3 *If the above technique is successful, and someone you know suddenly turns into someone you don't know, you must keep a firm grip on your sense of reality.*

You will probably do best to keep your vision to yourself, as it is very much your own experience and has little or no relevance to the person who you have been looking at. Many of the faces that people report having seen in this way are classic stereotype faces of different cultures, eg, Red Indians, Egyptians, or Chinese.

EXERCISE: *Clairvoyance 2*

Around the human head, all sorts of lights constantly swirl and flash. This is the human aura. It is a subject of study in itself and would require a book to itself, even to be partially understood and appreciated. As you become more aware psychically, this aura, particularly around the head (though it is present around all of the body), may break through into your ordinary day to day vision. It can appear as a kind of gentle yellow halo stretching about a foot from the head, or it may be seen as streaks or shafts of light raying out. In fact, your early impressions of lights around a head can be of almost any form, shape or colour. Sudden pink flashes, silver streaks, yellow flares in an upward direction, green fringes, or purple dots — all are possibilities — as are grey, red or black patches.

1 *Use the glancing technique as described above, or try this. Look straight past the head, and concentrate on not looking at the very thing you want to look at!*

2 *Over a period of time you will see some surprising phenomena.*

But once again try not to get too excited. For now, simply appreciate what you perceive, and resist any temptation to give great significance to your visions. They are for your own benefit, not for the purposes of peering into the souls of your fellows (as you might mistakenly imagine you are doing). It is possible to know certain things clairvoyantly from other people's auras, but the essential factor in that kind of psychic perception is that you should have the consent of whoever you are looking at, and that they should want to know and request to know what your perceptions are. For now, just see what you happen to see and try to leave it at that.

That's all about the head for the moment. As there will be a lot of observing in this chapter, let me tell you in more general terms how to turn your budding psychic perception on to your friends and colleagues. As I have said, the human body is a wonderful starting point for psychic observation. Looking at it is in many ways exactly like an exercise you did earlier when you looked at the candle. First you watched the flame, and then after you'd blown it out you were still able to hold and concentrate on an impression that remained behind inside you. It is the same sort of process with clairvoyant perception of the human body, but on a more mental level. The body is there for you to see in front of you but then instead of snuffing it out like a candle, you have to mentally close down your response to the external image, and remain inwardly balanced and sensitive to a different set of impressions.

These impressions will arise in you fleetingly at first but, with time, you will be able to grasp them for long enough to trust and hopefully enjoy them. It is the process of a lifetime, and you will always have to be updating and renewing your impressions of what is what, and what means what, so don't hurry! These psychic impressions are real, and will show soon enough. They should not be forced.

The other important thing about human watching from a psychic point of view is that, in a way, you are looking at yourself. All the powers, potential, and emotions that others bodies show, you have in you. You will remember if you did the head exercise above, where you imitated the movement of other heads, that you were able to arouse feelings in yourself that corresponded with the unspoken feelings of others. This you experienced as a result of becoming aware of the *movement* of their head. This idea of the movement, or a particular *energy* associated with a particular part of the body is revealing. From now on you are going to become very aware of the movements present in the various sections of the body. You must learn to feel the subtle movements or energies taking place within you.

For example, we noticed that in general the head has a kind of upward, thrusting, 'get to the top sort of movement'. It doesn't look right when it hangs downwards. Have you ever watched someone falling asleep sitting upright? As their consciousness slips away their head drops slowly forward. Then suddenly it battles upwards again, made aware by its own movement that it has lost control. Immediately it tries to summon fading consciousness back to where it thinks it should be! This battle is amusing to watch, especially if the performer is a person of apparently great external dignity or importance! Anyway, the point is, that it is by becoming sensitive to the various movements in our bodies that we can learn a lot about our deeper psychic tendencies . . . and I might add, as a complete side effect, the deeper tendencies of others. Now back to the parts of the body.

Head, hands and voice
The head is very much the leader of a team that makes up the top half of the body. Its other members are the hands, arms and voice, which are the head's main connection with the world outside. Whatever the head conceives it causes to happen in the physical world outside through the upper limbs, and voice. Therefore, let's view the upper half of the body as one being. A noisy articulate creature with a brain, and two symmetrical appendages sticking out one on either side for the purpose of doing what the head wants. Children's first drawings of humans look like this.

To the basic upwards movement of the head, voice and arms add an outwards and forwards movement. Try to feel these basic movements in your own limbs and speech. Once again, observing others will help.

It is very easy to see the two at work serving their ruler, the head, when we watch someone talking. Arms, hands and voice all perform an extremely complex dance of gestures and sounds, each with its specific meaning, and all used completely unconsciously. Perhaps you have had the experience of somebody talking to you when you were coming down with flu, or feeling unwell in some way, or perhaps even becoming drunk! Suddenly, you completely lose track of what the person is saying, and become hypnotized by the sight of their jaw going up and down and their hands and arms flapping about like branches in the wind! Direct your psychic concentration to this dance of sound and movement in as controlled a way as possible, to increase your powers of clairvoyance.

The subject of body language has been well explored, and different gestures are known to mean certain things. Similarly, inflections of the voice can also reveal things to a careful observer. However, this is not really what we are looking for in a psychic observation (though it plays its part). I want to direct you to something beyond psychological 'Manwatching'. Hidden in the subtle combinations of sound and movement of someone's voice, hands and head there lives a mood, a kind of spirit, to which you can open up. You can become aware of this mood within yourself, as you watch the 'dance' before you and, slowly but surely, insight into what is contained in this mood — sometimes very specific and worldly things — seeps into your awareness.

EXERCISE: *Speaking with a stranger*

Next time you speak with a stranger, as well as making the normal polite response and listening to what they say, try to concentrate on the movement of his/her voice, hands and head and ask yourself:

1 *Do the hands make certain movements in space with the voice.*

2 *Are they at work most when the voice is silent?*

3 *Does the voice make sharp quick sounds, or quiet flowing sounds?*

4 *Does the head seem to be in harmony with hands and voice?*

There are many such questions that I could suggest to you, but the psychic process is too quick for such a rational approach. In the end, as a result of something you have seen in a split second, your impressions will all boil down to a mood within yourself.

5 *Now here comes the main point of this exercise. Can you give this mood a label, using very few words — preferably only one?*

Keep your insight to yourself. Confidence will come with the slow steady strengthening of your inner moods, not from asking the person under study to confirm whether your perception of their inner state is accurate. This could be socially disastrous! So concentrate on clarifying your one or two word perception and never ask for confirmation. If your feeling is strong, and clear, it will be right!

EXERCISE: *Analyzing the voice*

There is an occult theory that if you could simultaneously give voice to all the sounds that the human voice can speak, you would speak a human shape!

Our ability to create sounds in the air around us, to express our deepest feelings, is of such great psychic significance that it is hard to direct a newcomer without advising them first to read several books on the subject, to experiment, listen and completely rethink their perception of life!

Sounds spoken by humans can awaken deep responses to the listener. The procession of vowels and consonants, the timing of the words as they flow, and the rise or fall of each syllable, all can evoke a wealth of insight. And give power too. Human sound is truly magic . . . it is as if by speaking, people really do bring things into existence.

Try to follow this exercise in your own way.

1 *The next time you hear some short statement, preferably one that doesn't require a response from you, select from it a phrase, just a few words that particularly catch your ear. The meaning of the chosen words is of little importance, but once you have chosen them, stay with them until you have reached a conclusion.*

2 *At the same time, bear in mind that talking breaks down into simple sounds: ah, oo, ee, tuh, duh, guh and so on. Concentrate on one sound, say 'oo', you will find it evokes in you a certain feeling. Another sound, 'ee', will perhaps produce an altogether different feeling.*

This difference is subtle, so you will have to repeat the sounds to yourself and look quite hard inside for these feelings at first. In time, each sound can give you a distinct feeling. Most people can appreciate the difference between the feeling of a 'ssss' and that of a 'guh'. Or the difference between long musical vowels like 'a' (as in hay), 'oh' (as in road), or 'oo' (as in food), and the short sharp consonants, like 't' 'k' 'b', etc. Just to clarify this idea of the mood of sound, consider the following.

A succession of consonants invokes an official or brainy feeling both in the speaker and in the listener. Simply saying the following, sentence, for example, regardless of whether it means anything in your life, produces a mood: 'We are instructed to keep each particle strictly separate.'

On the other hand, a long string of vowels gives a dreamy poetic feel. 'We all saw only rolling snow and moonlight.' In fact, some people find it hard to utter certain vowel sounds at all, because of the feelings they have when so doing. Becoming aware of these fundamental sound feelings is the first purpose of this exercise.

3 *Now, go back to the short sample of speech you overheard. Hopefully, it is held in your sound memory as a series of the above described basic sound feelings.*

Laid over them, and distorting them slightly, is a unique pattern and colouring given to them by the particular voice box that expressed them. Apply all your sensitivity to detecting this added pattern, and then feel in yourself the mood it contained.

This exercise is very much like the earlier one in which you were discriminating between live sound, and sound that came from the mineral world. The only real difference is in the depth of soul feeling and amount of information present in even the smallest sounds of human speech. Even single syllables open up to reveal layer upon layer of psychic content. Simply stay with a sound, perhaps repeating it to yourself and let it reveal what it contains. This sounds very complex, but it takes just a split second to do, and it will also provide a rich insight into your own sound making habits. Finally, try to distill your sound mood impressions down into only one or two short, sharp key words. You must remember to do this vital last stage of the exercise, or you run the risk of becoming very confused after a short while. Not to quickly label these intuitions at the end would be a bit like delicately shepherding a herd of jumpy sheep into their pen, and then not closing the gate!

Your psychic experience should never confuse you, rather, it should cause wonder and openness. If your psychic feelings are real to you, you need have no fear about slapping a quick label on to them for storage purposes.

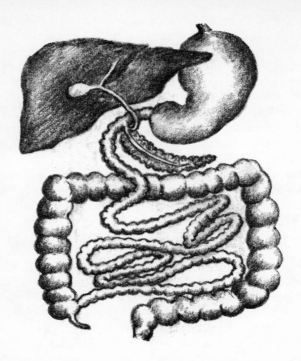

The trunk: Heart, lungs, spine, and intestines

The next part of the body to focus on is the trunk, including the chest, heart and lungs, and the stomach and intestines. All very solid and, on the face of it, not the stuff of psychic awareness you might think. More a region for doctors, surgeons, and anatomy students. Not so. If you can see this a certain way you will considerably enhance your understanding.

At the centre of this 'trunk' creature, acting as its brain, is your second 'brain' — the spinal column. The spine is the brain and nerve centre of this fleshy central region, and is really an extension of your head. Also, it behaves in much the same way! It strives to hold everything where it wants it, it regulates a team of organs, and it plays a great part in the struggle upwards. It can also prove to be another considerable source of aching!

There is one big difference though, the spine has no direct way of making itself felt in the outside world, so it is not anywhere near as megalomaniacal. The kingdom it rules over is much more internal and earth bound. Furthermore, it doesn't deal in thoughts, it deals in immediate unconscious impulses.

EXERCISE: Measured steps

This is designed to help you to become aware of the kind of messages that operate in this region. Do use your commonsense with this one.

1 *Stand with your back to the edge of a* shallow *drop, or pond or something of that nature that you would not like to slip into. Place your heels right at the very edge. (Please DO NOT try this in a risky way and fall off a cliff or into a raging torrent or something!)*

2 *Take four paces forward, counting them off as you step each pace.*

3 *Now take four steps backward!*

'It's quite safe,' your head will tell you. 'No problem. Simply walk carefully backwards four slightly smaller steps and you will be OK. You've measured it out, so there is no chance of falling into the pond,' (or whatever you have behind you). With this in mind, you take your four steps backwards.

At about step number three you may become aware of a distinctly different impulse building up in your body. A kind of paralysis starting in your trunk and back, and flowing into your legs. It brings everything to an unwilling standstill. You will have to use a lot of head to overcome it, if you can at all. It doesn't matter how carefully you measure your steps or tell yourself it is safe, a powerful impulse will arise within your middle area and back every time.

Imagination
Visualize this powerful trunk being an entity in itself quite separate from the rest of your body (not an easy thing to do, I'll admit). You will get the picture of a sturdy, enclosed sort of creature, with a lot of warm movement going on inside. It knows its place and though it has no direct connection of its own with the outside world, via any senses of its own, it is kept busy processing the material world that it encounters. It keeps the head creature on top of it supplied and happy. In many ways it's a bit like a cow. There are three main energy movements to be felt in this creature:

The movement of the breath.

The movement of the blood.

The movement of various secretory glands.

All three are full of psychic significance.

The heart and lungs are, above all, rhythmic feelings. They set a pulse for the whole human race. The ratio of heart beat to lungs, in a relaxed state is about four to one. Four heart beats to one in/out cycle of the breath . . . the basic four pulse of much music.

Although an inner thing, the heart-lung rhythm is very much linked to the outer world, via the head, and there is a constant dialogue and influencing of the one upon the other. The head stimulates hurried breathing or hot flushes when certain external situations arise. And the lungs in turn supply only the necessary fraction of the usual oxygen supply to the brain, when it is unconscious.

Perhaps the most interesting thing about lung and heart movement is that it is perpetual. As long as you are alive — awake or asleep — heart and lungs are with you, energized and active. These two are *never* absent. Your consciousness however, can come and go; it can leave you for days or even years.

EXERCISE: *Feel your pulse beat*

A *very quick one. Simply feel your own pulse (in your wrist), and count how many beats you can feel per breath.*

All these ideas I am putting forward not simply as interesting facts, but as things you can experience for yourself as a result of tuning-in to the feel of the subtler movements of your body. The experience of sensing your breath energy ebbing and flowing is at the centre of a whole realm of psychic awakening. The feeling of your blood coursing through you is a link with a great mystery of existence.

The diaphragm
The lower area of the trunk is completely separated off from the rhythmic organs by a powerful sheet of muscle called the diaphragm. It is a world entirely of its own, having no sensory connection with the outside. This is the dark interior into which many of us have a natural (for this age) aversion to looking! A place of intestines, strange gurgling noises, smells, and a whole excretery dimension that is almost impossible to write about without offending people. The sex organs are here and, more discussable but less

well known perhaps, our centre of balance (the pelvis and hips) is centred here. This area is a powerhouse of movement and energy.

It is highly likely that your energies here are not flowing as well as they could. This lower part of us is not listened to or appreciated as well as it should be in order to ensure good psychic health. We are so much 'head' people, that we tend to take our guts for granted, happily imposing on them the rhythms, ideas and energies of the top end. This one-way forced communication causes the lower energies great frustration. Gut movement is kept down so much that when it does burst through it often shows in a rush, and makes itself felt upstairs in the head in a sudden and distorted way. The mental impressions it creates can be dramatic or even violent. I'm sure you know the experience of nightmares after going to bed on a full stomach.

Disruptive and uncomfortable psychic sensations also, too often, arise from the misdirection of these hugely powerful 'stomach' forces. Many practising psychics draw on these energies deliberately, frequently producing successful and spectacular results, though sometimes at the expense of their own long-term comfort and well being.

All in all, the situation here in the body is a bit like that at large in the world. We are dependent on Mother Nature and the planet for our physical nourishment. Yet we impose ourselves on them, exploit them, and even pollute them, in a shortsighted urge to fulfil plans that we have decided in our heads we want to achieve.

The movements of this region have a different pace from heart and lung rhythm. It is more of a constant cycle than a regular beat. For our own psychic benefit (if for no other) we must learn to listen closely to the movements and energies here in the lower trunk.

Older people will know well how the tendency to doze after eating becomes more and more irresistible as time depletes youthful liveliness. This is a good example of gut wisdom coming through positively. Energy is withdrawn from the head (often unwillingly), and the lower forces do their steady work undisturbed. In return, many people find that the thoughts and reflections that come into their heads during this period of quiet digestion have a deeper, more intuitive quality than they would have had if they had been moving about, following active ideas and urges.

EXERCISE: Basic rhythms

For this exercise you will require one beetroot, and a certain amount of wholesome curiosity. This chapter is largely about body movements, and the word 'movement' takes on a certain double meaning in this context of bowels and intestines. It is well known, that excreting and secreting plays a large part in many darker operations of the occult world. Primitive magic is well aware of the powerful energies inherent in these natural processes. We, as people wishing to grow clairvoyantly, need have nothing whatsoever to do with dark forces, but in our attempts to get in touch with the natural movements of the lower half of our trunk must try to see the relevance of getting to know its basic feel. Being psychic is not exclusively a head experience. It is a feeling of the whole body. So try this!

Your body has what is called a 'passage time', that is, the time taken for a quantity of liquid to pass right through the digestive system and out. Most of us simply put things in at one end, and make very little connection between that, and what comes out the other end. So:

1 *Cut up the beetroot and boil it until you have about a pint or more of scarlet liquid.*

2 *Let it cool, then transfer it to a glass and drink as much of it as you can (bearing in mind your health, comfort, and a large measure of common sense). Note the time.*

3 *At the point afterwards when your urine takes on a pinkish hue, you will have some insight into the timing of one of the most basic rhythms of your body!*

I make no suggestions as to ways of experiencing the cycle of solids as they pass through you. Experiment as you feel comfortable or not. Certainly, there are psychic lessons and feelings to be experienced in all of this very basic physical sensation, when it is a part of a sincere programme of psychic development. In the next chapter I deal with natural rhythms of a different kind.

The hips and sex organs
The lowest section of the trunk is the hips and sex organs area. The essentialness of not letting the energies get blocked applies here too. So much power is locked up here that there is very little scope in such a short book to do it justice. Whole schools of philosophy and psychology are devoted to trying to explain and integrate the

urges that flow outwards from this area. What's more, the male and female sensations are quite different. All I can sensibly say here is as follows.

Just as you attempt to become aware of the movements and feel of the other body regions: your thoughts, lungs and gut, so you should try to become aware of the movements and feel of your sexual and reproductive region. Once again, as in a lot of psychic phenomena, your head is your main enemy, always seeking to impose its own inner deadness and immobility on everything. The essential quality of the hips is to move in a flowing balancing way, and the nature of sex energy is unconscious and without need for thought. Inevitably, this area will be in conflict with our head urges, so we must try to understand it.

Most of us, particularly men, are afraid to move our hips as fully as we can. We are stiff and locked in this area, and it can be seen in the way we walk and position ourself when standing. Polite people in our society keep pelvic movements to a minimum, and many energies are thus prevented from escaping and flowing. Try to feel your own psychic situation around your hips and buttocks. See what you can sense about your movements or lack of them.

Sexual organs have an energy of their own, separate from the hip balancing movement. Their energy is to do with reproduction and the whole cycle of bringing a new human body into existence out of two separate ones. You will need to search deeply within yourself to grasp this energy. It is very subtle and powerful.

EXERCISE: Let's dance

Another very simple one. Next time you get the opportunity . . .

1 *Dance, preferably, in the modern way.*

There is an atmosphere of great tolerance these days on most dance floors, and the sight of even the stiffest, oldest and 'straightest' person making their bodily contribution raises no eyebrows. Obviously, there is a lot of shyness and embarrassment in those of us who are not great movers, so don't create problems by forcing yourself to leap about in the hope that it will improve your psychic powers!

2 *Simply, if you get a chance to move about anonymously on a crowded dance floor, take it . . . and give those hips a wiggle. You will feel the effect of the tiniest hip wiggle all over, even in places you had forgotten existed.*

You should by now have a distinct picture in your mind of this middle 'creature' of your body, and the sort of things it feels and does. Try to picture all of the creatures you have seen so far, happily sitting, one on top of the other and working in harmony.

A word about auras

The trunk region often displays clear colourful phenomena, especially in people of strong character (strong good or strong bad, it really doesn't matter). Be prepared to see colours such as green or orange from the occasional person and, more often shafts of red and black. Be content to see whatever you might. Resist the temptation to attach critical or flattering judgmental interpretations. Body auras can be a clear source of medical diagnosis, but this psychic skill must be learned patiently from a live teacher rather than from a book.

Legs and bottom

The last basic body area, to concentrate your attention on is the legs and bottom. This also includes the hips.

This area or animal, if you can picture it as such, from the hips down to the feet, is mainly concerned with running and walking. It is composed largely of levers and rods, designed for dealing with and climbing over the material world. Like the other body creatures, it has a brain which is also a vital psychic centre. The nerve centre of this being is located in the region known as the solar plexus, around the pit of the stomach.

As you develop clairvoyantly, your solar plexus will become the seat of your psychic sensitivity. It is an area to get to know. Whereas the gut energies were very powerful and hard to control, the movement of this solar plexus area is much more refined and sympathetic − and a more sociable psychic organ! Its great strength becomes apparent when you use it to empathize with or tune in to other human beings. Later on, when you begin to try out your powers of psychic insight on other people, you will become very aware of this sensitive area. Physically, it is actually quite hard to define, but as it is not really a physical organ for our purposes, this is not so important. Try to get the feel of an energy around your stomach area that isn't digestive, and isn't sexual.

The legs might seem at first glance to be not particularly fruitful for psychic purposes, as their function is so mechanical. But even they have an element of magic. Everything that the body does, reveals something of the spirit that is influencing the part brought into use. The walking motion of the legs when observed on its own, actually reveals a lot about the content of the head. Also, there is something comic about the way disembodied legs move on their own from the waist down. Legs are always potentially funny! (There is something about the idea of a Ministry of Silly Walks that somehow seems a real possibility!)

The basic walk movement breaks down into three separate energies:

A starting off lifting energy.

A sustained carrying energy.

A placing energy.

This lifting, carrying and placing is totally unconscious, but it reveals in us deeper attitudes about ourselves and how we show what we feel about ourselves to the outside world. Think about it, and feel what exactly you are doing in your own walk. Do you lift your leg high and quickly, or slowly, hardly getting it off the ground? Do you carry it directly and straight or does it flap about left and right, or perhaps require the support of the earth, and scrape along? When you place it down, is it with a solid and assertive bang of the heel, or gently and with timidity on the toe?

There are infinite variations of nuance in these three phases of leg movement in walking. It is amazing to see what some people do with their legs! Watch them for a while and you will find that the movements speak of the most mixed attitudes to the physical world, and give rise to many strange and wonderful feelings in you.

EXERCISE: Footprints

Although I recommend it, it is surprisingly hard to watch people walking. There is so much else going on simultaneously, that by the time you have tuned in to the subtleties of their gait, they have disappeared out of view! People simply do not stay in one place while they are walking; it is most inconvenient!

One of the best ways I know of tuning in to a walk is:

1 *Go to a wet sandy beach, or wait until it snows, and get a friend to walk ahead of you for a few yards.*

2 *Then catch them up, putting your feet accurately in the deep footprints.*

Doing this, even if you have developed only a slight psychic awareness, can bring on quite powerful feelings of rapport with your friend's inner rhythms and emotions. Stepping in the footprints of strangers, however, has a curiously uncomfortable quality, and I don't recommend it. Try it once though.

For watching the three-fold movement, there is no substitute for following as close behind your subject as possible, and imitating him/her. This is a socially difficult manoeuvre, as you can well imagine, and can result in embarrassment if not handled delicately, so go easy.

The feet

Feet, it may surprise many people to know, are psychically highly charged. So highly charged in fact, that I am going to have to leave them out in a detailed way. I hope you can discover for yourself, the implications of these organs. In our shoe-clad society there's not a lot you can do to increase foot awareness, so it is best to let foot understanding grow of its own accord as a result of psychic expansion elsewhere.

However, a good foot massage from a *competent* foot masseur can take you on a journey around your body and all its feelings in the space of an hour! It is an experience to be recommended and will

take you a long way towards insight into the specialized and powerful potential present in your feet.

Eastern cultures retain a great reverence for the spiritual possibilities of feet and are quite physical in the way they express their foot consciousness. We in the West have become more verbal and symbolic in our attitudes to feet! To set about recovering our lost foot awareness in any practical way would involve a lot of discarding of shoes — social suicide! Here are a few perspectives though. For shoes, read feet:

Many an actor in the world of theatre who is having difficulty in getting into the right 'feel' of a new character has discovered the essence of the role immediately upon putting on a certain pair of shoes. It seems that if the feet feel right the rest of the character drops into place.

Many people upon first seeing a baby, feel a strong urge to touch, kiss or even 'nibble' its feet. And they often do!

It is easy to build up a detailed mental image of someone you know, if you place their shoes in front of you, in the sort of position that their feet would take up if actually wearing the shoes. Seeing the shoes gives rise to an entire bodily picture.

I have a friend who, when frightened, nervous, or in awe of someone, looks at that person's shoes! She says it makes them seem more human and vulnerable. There is something endearing about even the most important person's shoes.

Your foot is your connection with the mineral element of the earth, and your body energies do not stop at the foot (just as they do not start at the head). They flow through the foot, giving and taking from the ground beneath you. The feet of holy persons have always been recognized as a source of great power, so there *is* a lot to be learned from these literally down to earth, sometimes rather smelly, and apparantly non-psychic members. See what you can find.

I hope now you have in your mind the image of these body 'creatures', one on top of the other, out of which your body is made. It is a distinctly non-scientific view, and is intended to promote psychic experiment, rather than to convince the sceptical. There is much more that could be said, so feel free to research. Head learning from books will eventually filter down into your other centres if it contains suitable ideas. More could also be said about such things as the aura, both around the head and the body, but I hope there is here food enough for reflection — to touch and inspire your growing psychic perceptions.

7

SLEEP, DREAMS, AND THE RHYTHM OF LIFE

In our attempts to develop our powers of clairvoyance, until the next chapter at least, we are concentrating on looking at what we already have, rather than searching for a sixth sense, which we then set out to master. This is because I want your psychic growth to be natural, and easy. We all have within us the abilities of perceiving things in a psychic way; it is really a simple matter of getting used to using what is already there. This chapter, largely about sleep, is a perfect example; if there is one thing that everyone does plenty of it's this humble activity of snoozing. But what a rich area for psychic growth this easy period of apparent nothingness is. Sleep is a gift to the enquiring psyche as well as rest to the physical body.

Many of us I am sure have heard of dramatic sounding psychic jargon such as 'trance mediumship', 'altered states of consciousness', 'out of body experience', 'transcendental awareness' etc. It may come as a surprise to know that every one of us experiences these seemingly difficult achievements nightly, without the slightest pride or self-consciousness! As we snuggle under the covers, and drift off into the land of nod, we are in fact crossing over a mysterious threshold into a psychic realm, every bit as real as the physical, everyday one we know so well.

We take sleep so much for granted: the entire human race performs this regular act of closing down and mentally going off somewhere else and yet, as a phenomenon of our personal lives, it is amazing how little comment it raises. It is simply brushed aside as normal, while we get on with the busy achievements of day-to-day living. In this section, a major step for your psychic growth will be to start looking at sleep differently. Like so much of what we have learned earlier we will find that our psychic way of seeing is completely in conflict with the so-called normal, or sensible point of view. So, be prepared to turn your brain around.

Look at it this way. If you were married to a person who regularly kept disappearing to some apparently irresistible place, and then just as regularly reappeared, looking bright and refreshed a few hours later, you would not rest until you knew exactly what was going on in this mysterious place! The space of absence would take on a great importance. You wouldn't just brush it off, I'm sure!

Or perhaps you've had an experience similar to the following. You are out late. It is four o'clock in the morning, the dead of night, and you are walking through a residential area. The quietness is overwhelming. The least psychically sensitive person can immediately notice the atmosphere of night. Something different is happening. Even the late-late crowd have finally gone to sleep! Within the enclosing walls of the houses, whole families, their noise and business of the day completely forgotten, are tucked up in bed, horizontal and unconscious, unaware and completely vulnerable. Something in the stillness and darkness seems to protect and enfold the oblivious humanity. The depth of night has a powerful and unique feel of its own. Frequently, people only become aware of the reality of this enveloping night-silence, when they experience a sudden wild urge to shatter it, loudly!

Our day-to-day minds play tricks on us and delude us easily. When we look back over a period of time — say a week — in our memory, we edit out the periods of sleep. We give the picture a totally artificial impression of unity, stringing together the bright daytime bits. The resulting sequence we then hold to our hearts as a true representation of what we experience during that period. In fact, it is only edited highlights! It's only half of what happened. This tendency to perceive only half of what is going on is a natural obstacle brought on by the 'bright light' what-you-see-is-what-you-get-feel of these material times.

Becoming aware of this tendency to notice only half of what is available, then slowly to set about opening up to the other half, will bring on a dramatic enrichment of your psychic perception.

Two basic realms of experience

In Chapter Two, I drew your attention to the existence of two basic realms of experience. I called them the man-made and the natural (god-made) worlds. I'm sorry if anyone feels uneasy about the word 'god'. To get the best out of the exercises in this chapter, we must decide which department we fit into! The answer, surely, has to be god-made. Whether city dweller or country dweller, whether we work in a computer room or outside on the land, whether we live on micro-wave TV dinners, or organic brown rice, we all belong in the god-made department and are sustained by Nature. This is important to realize in the matter of your psychic growth.

No matter what you do or say in your daily life, and no matter what rhythm your lifestyle sets for you, when it comes to your inner clairvoyant nature, you are always going to be subject to the rules of a different, more 'God' governed system. Psychic forces flow according to the rhythms of the earth, the sun, the moon and the stars, regardless of what we do about our individual lives on a day-to-day level.

Imagine this slightly exaggerated scene. A man wakes from sleep at the sound of a digital alarm, eats his processed breakfast food in a centrally heated home. He gets into the car (via an internal garage door) and drives to the underground parking lot beneath his office block. From there, he goes up in the lift to the tenth floor and takes a seat in front of a computer terminal that connects him to the other side of the world. After six or seven hours of this he returns to his insulated home, perhaps noticing as he puts on the windscreen wipers that it is raining, or maybe thinking to himself as he walks in and turns on the lights that the nights are starting to draw in. In such ways, even the most urban person has woven into their life the rhythms of nature. With a little perception, you can see the beat of the planet underlying even the most sophisticated city lifestyles.

All of which brings me back to the business of only really being aware of half of our reality. For a creature who regularly 'loses' its awareness of itself in sleep, only being half aware is quite understandable. Actually we are all too mentally tuned in to the Sun.

Creatures of the dark

Until we discover our psychic state of mind, it is our daylight awake consciousness that give meaning to our life. But think for a second if there was no such thing as sleep. If there was no time at all in our lives when we were 'not there', as in sleep. If we just experienced one unbroken sequence of awakeness. We would not be aware of being alive to anywhere near the extent we are as a result of having our life as it were regularly removed from us. It is the dark patches in between that makes us feel we are awake in the daylight hours. Darkness makes us more aware of ourselves as individuals than light does. We are very much creatures of the dark, and sleep seems to hold some big secrets.

And there is another factor to be considered here too. Our whole life is defined by a darkness at the front, by darkness at the end. We come into life itself out of a darkness, a void that feels very much like the non-existence of sleep. If we remember our life back as far as we can go we reach a blackness, within which we can feel that we might have our origin. It is sensible to feel this. There is a clear logic in looking for more of something by peering into the place just before the place where we found the bit we've got! There is a happy attractiveness in the idea, that there is some lost part of us present in sleep.

The sun, however, drives out darkness and all ideas of it. It is the most noticeable thing in the world. No one can miss the sun's positive qualities. Always, it grabs and monopolizes our attention, leaving no room for vague possibilities. When the sun shines it is as if the stars don't exist, and so powerful is its suggestion that even many adults are surprised when you point out that the stars are shining up there all the time, even at lunch time! They forget that the stars are in the sky always. For a second their sun logic deserts them as they realize that somewhere inside them they must actually believe that stars only exist at night!

In the awareness of the sun there is only one way of seeing things, no mysteries. And until it is pointed out that there are other rhythms and forces, the undisputed bright power of the sun is master, spreading its influence outwards. Darkness comes to be regarded as an empty space within which we do nothing more than wait for the reappearance of the all powerful light. This 'awake-or-nothing-at-all' attitude pervades our whole view of ourselves. Just as the sun blinds us to the view of the stars in the day so it also deadens us to other, twilight — but still natural — types of awareness that are just as real.

EXERCISE: The full story

Just to consider how deep runs our belief that our sun awareness is the entire picture, do this:

1 *Imagine a plant. But what you have probably imagined is not a plant at all. It is only half a plant! What you have quite naturally imagined in your head in response to the word 'plant' is actually a thing that does not exist anywhere in creation. You have almost certainly forgotten to include the root section.*

2 *Now imagine a tree and I'm sure the same will occur. You will see a trunk, branches and leaves.*

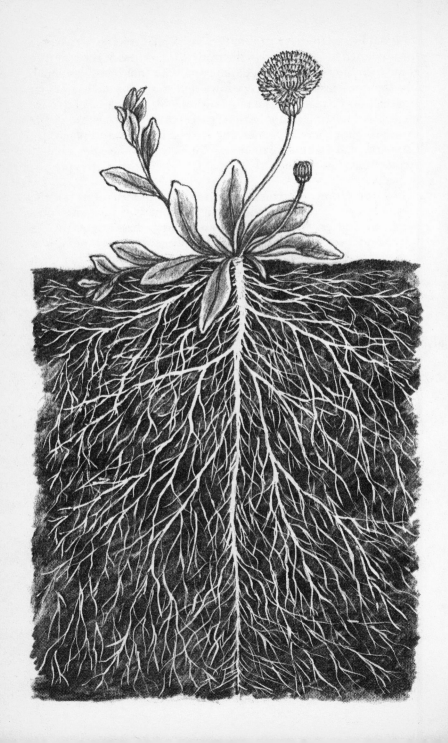

If I want you to see a whole tree, I will have to explain this in detail, because the word 'tree' otherwise only means the visible part of a tree!

Plants and trees all have in reality at least half of them as roots.

In fact, many are more present in the invisible world underground than they are in the bright upper world, yet this fact is simply not recognized. The whole pattern of our thinking and language is so dominated by our senses, and our senses are dominated overwhelmingly by the sun.

In sleep, we move into a different kingdom where the forces of the sun cannot enter. We enter a world where our external physical senses can be of no use to us. To experience what is present in this other world we must awaken our psychic sense organs. The exercises throughout this book so far, have been designed to do just that, so you should already have it in your power to see at least a few faint glimmers of this inner world during your nightly visits.

Sleep and dreams

Let me point out a few things about the night and time rhythms in general. Time is very much a natural resource, like air or water. The way we feel time is by rhythm, and cycles of rhythm link us all together in a deep way. Whether you measure time by a clock, or simply feel it passing within you, it is the same now as it has always been.

It is interesting to note that household electric lighting has only been with us for a mere hundred years. Before that there was oil-based lighting, but only for the rich; and before that even, it was a case of when the sun goes down you go to sleep or sit in the dark (more or less). Our ability to ignore the rhythm of light and darkness set by nature is a very recent addition to our lifestyles. It is not hard to return a short distance back in time, and appreciate the simplicity of an earlier rhythm. Try it. Then, the sun ruled the day and the moon and stars ruled the night. If we want to grow psychically we must find a deep affinity with these facts, and tune in to these rhythms. Obviously, I'm not suggesting you change your lifestyle dramatically. I merely recommend you to open up to these ideas and then see how you feel.

Different times of day have different qualities and feels to them. For example, morning is good for brain work, and afternoon is good for hand tasks. This quality of day does not make itself felt because of what you decide to do in your personal routine. Probably quite the reverse. There is every chance that your routine has evolved as an unconscious response by you to feelings inherent in the hour.

EXERCISE: *Passage of the hours*

1 *Sit down quietly and decide what parts a day is divided into.
Think carefully and try to pinpoint exactly when the feel of one
period turns into a different mood.*

For example, when does morning start to feel like afternoon? (Don't
say at twelve o'clock! That would be totally theoretical.) Or, when
do you start to feel you are approaching evening meal time? Is 'afternoon' split up into several sections that somehow feel different?

2 *Try to find the mood of the various times of the day and note
how they follow in sequence. Is there one time you like more
than another? How does your favourite time of day feel?*

3 *You won't be able to think about this for long, because
concentration isn't easy, so why not ask a friend what they think
about the various times of day, and which ones they prefer.*

People are all very different, so don't try to win anyone over to your
way of feeling. The passage of the hours is a very personal thing; a
bit like a person's choice of politics or religion!

4 *While you are at it, decide which days of the week feel best, and
why.*

What mood does each one have? For example, is Thursday better than Wednesday? And what can be done about Sunday to make it a bit more like Friday? State your likes and dislikes boldly.

The Moon — Queen of the night

The last exercise, though revealing, still keeps you very much in contact with the sun, as the hours, and the day itself, are so dominated by the movement of the sun. To develop further into the rhythm most appropriate for psychic development, we must begin to get to know the ruler of the kingdom of night, the moon. Try to establish a practical and physical relationship between yourself and the moon! Let me explain why.

For most of us, the moon is just this thing up in the sky that we see from time to time. As far as we know it just appears now and then in different places, and in different shapes without any real rhyme or reason. In truth, though, the moon has a very profound and rhythmic movement, and it is to this that we could well turn our attention. Get to know the ways of the moon as consciously as you can. Believe me, the more you start to notice all the details of the moon in a very specific personal way . . . what it does, where and when, the more a force from within you will rise to the surface as clairvoyant ability and insight. Try and see.

EXERCISE: Moon watching

Reading books about the moon is a distinctly second-rate form of moon study. Watching it over the weeks is best, although it is a difficult thing to start, as it is so hard to know what is going on. Clouds are the main problem at first in these latitudes, and sometimes the moon simply seems to disappear, or if it's there you forget where it was when you last saw it. Altogether, the whole thing seems impossible, meaningless and most unrhythmical! All this is normal. But if you persist in your moon watching you will discover things along the following lines. The moon rises and sets just as the sun does. The moon moves across the sky at night.

1 *Find out where north, south, east and west are, in relation to your house, or you won't know how to remember or predict where the moon is going to rise or set.*

Unlike the sun, the moon will rise on different sides of the house at

different times. Most of us can usually remember where the sunset or sunrise will be . . . something like 'over the trees in the back garden'. But not so with the moon. It has more choices. One night it could disappear behind the chimney pots over the road, and the next time you look for it, it could be setting over the roof of the house next door, or even behind the factory at the far end of the street.

2 *Spend time getting to know its ways in relation to your local personal geography, so that you can see its rhythm.*

3 *In your observations, be personal, and subjective!*

If you saw the woman next door getting ready for bed last Thursday and the moon was shining just over from her house between the vegetable patch and the place where Granny slipped and fell, well remember it like that. Avoid astronomical jargon. Declination, waxing phases, waning phases, the quarters and so on are all perfectly valid once you have got some inner feeling of your own to pin these ideas on to. They can otherwise make you feel very objective and important and spoil the whole business. The moon changes shape as the days pass. Depending on where you start noticing it, it gets smaller, nightly, disappears completely, then gets slowly bigger until it is huge and noticeable again for a while. Then starts its cycle all over.

The dark portion that is hidden is on the left as the moon grows fuller, and on the right as it gets smaller. Why this happens you can find out in detail from an astronomy book if you wish. It is fascinating, not at all complicated, and will help you to find where the moon rises and sets.

4 *For the purposes of your psychic impressions and insights, the moon is your pulse, your basic beat. The period of one month, one lunar cycle is the single smallest interval of time.*

waxing   waning

You can not say you understand or have really digested a psychic impression until it has been a part of you for one lunar cycle. If you get a calendar with the phases of the moon marked on it, you will immediately see that the moon does not move according to the monthly divisions named on the calendar. It has a monthly pulse that crosses these calendar months.

The seasons: rhythm of the stars

There is one further rhythm that I would like to point out to you: the rhythm of the stars. You may have noticed that at certain times of the year some constellations are not visible in the sky. More likely though you haven't noticed this. Why should you? Who wants to spend freezing winter nights staring skywards through rain? However, if you do get curious and begin to notice only one basic reality about the movement of the heavens, you will realize that the earth actually has a rhythmic relationship with the stars. They don't just shine there every night, the same stars in the same places fixed and static. They have a rhythm too, and it is felt here on earth in the changing of the seasons.

Its sequence is a bit like that of the sun. In sun rhythm, day turns into twilight and twilight turns into night; night turns into dawn, and dawn turns into day again. With the star-rhythm, summer turns into autumn, and autumn turns into winter; winter turns into spring, and spring turns into summer again. Each season has its mood, and we must learn to feel these moods for what they are. We human beings are deeply embedded in this rhythm.

Naturally, to our sun-dominated way of looking at things there is a great tendency to throw this equal and symmetrical cycle completely off balance, and to think in terms of either winter or summer. We don't stop there either. Having put all the emphasis on summer and winter, we then unconsciously decide again, and eliminate winter in its own right! Something inside us selects summer as the main event, and everything is seen in terms of that! Winter is regarded as nothing more than a build up to summer. It is reduced (like night) to the status of a cold and empty time when nothing really is happening, and if anything is happening, it is only in preparation for glorious summer.

The forces of winter are deep and powerful, and in many senses are more awake than bright summer wakefulness. Think how vivid night's dreams can be, yet they have nothing to do with daytime sensory experience.

There are many forms of consciousness apart from being awake and thinking. For our psychic well being we should try to right the balance. Try to look closely at the moods of the forgotten seasons, particularly autumn and winter.

Have you noticed around September time, when all the schools open, so many people often start to think about taking night courses or enrolling in some improving activity? Feelings of reflection and an inward-looking mood take hold. Self-understanding rather than outside activities becomes important. You could compare this season to twilight. There are those who admit that they don't like twilight, the seam between night and day. It arouses in them disturbing reactions rather like those that they have when seeing a Tarot Pack for the first time. It alters their perspective. Something inward, deep, and with a will of its own is invoked. As I said before, if you can get in touch with this feeling so much the better, as it is the first stirrings of a real psychic awareness.

Begin to be aware that, as summer falls asleep into autumn, something in its own right awakens in winter. Something in nature and in us is awakened. Please remember this. Psychically speaking, winter is a time of waking up. The budding and flowering of summer is a very physical process, but it is in winter that those spiritual forces lying behind these displays can be seen clearly defined, against a less busy background.

Like a long and vivid dream, the forces of winter awake. Seen on the daily cycle, winter is the equivalent of the profound mental processes of deep sleep. Untouched by the demanding forces of the sun, the inner forces are free to pursue their subtle and mysterious patterns. Winter is a time of significant inner activity.

spring   summer

Dreaming

Our dream life can be more dramatic and interesting than our waking routine. We get up to the most amazingly varied things: fly, travel to exotic places, make love to any number of different partners, meet people, perform actions, and provoke reactions from the creatures and beings that populate our dream landscape. We have arguments, appear on stage, and sometimes walk about stark naked! Dreams are a rich source of experience, and even at its most unreal, a dream is always real enough to think about!

The problem, of course, arises when we want to know what our dreams mean. Our mental processes are set up in a one way only arrangement; we easily carry information from this physical world into our dreams, but getting something meaningful out of the dream and into our waking consciousness takes practice. It is a bit like the remembering backwards exercise of Chapter One. We have to reckon with the powerful, forward-looking forces of our heads. It can be done though.

You must approach your dream in the full certainty that there is something in it that you can use, understand, and apply in your daily life. It is a valid part of your experience. It is relevant, just like

autumn   winter

a conversation with the man next door, or a trip to the Sahara desert would be. You must bring something from it back into your waking life. An understanding, insight or even the smallest realization about this world that you can take closely to your heart, must arise in you as a result of thinking about your dreamworld. It really is not enough simply to marvel or recount how strange or even disturbing it was. You must try to find out exactly what, after your stay in this amazingly different domain, you are supposed to carry back with you and use. That is the meaning of your dream.

An old tradition says that by day you hurl your questions at the sun, and by night you listen for an answer — from the moon. Praying for a dream was, and still is, a tribal custom of the North American Indians. If a dream appears, it is embraced with great reverence and gratitude, and reflected upon privately until its meaning becomes clear. The Old Indians stated that if you wanted to get an answer back from the moon, you had first to ask the sun.

Similarly today, if we want to get something comprehensible out of our dream life we have first to put something specific in. Perhaps a question. The process requires a little faith to get it going, and this is a feature of all psychic practices. You have to believe you are looking in roughly the right quarters before you will be able to find what is there.

In terms of dreams, you must feel that your dream life can supply you with specific answers. Then ask your question. It is not enough to look at past dreams into which you have put nothing specific, in the hope of getting answers. At best, reflecting on such dream material will usually only tell you what questions you are asking yourself in your waking life. Then confusion and complication set in because you start unwittingly forcing and distorting these questions until they seem more like answers!

So, first your question must be strong enough to reach its goal and give an answer. It is also essential that you sincerely feel that you are addressing your question to a source that is capable of providing an answer. That is why I'm emphasizing this simple act of faith to get you going. Formulate a specific and clear question, and request a dream that will provide you with something you can understand and use in your life. Simply doing this will work wonders.

The language of dreams is pictures, and picture thinking is one of the first stages of psychic growth you learned in Chapter Three. However, dream pictures are notoriously hard to remember. By the time you have been awake a few seconds, your mind has built an elaborate barrier blocking out all but the faintest echoes of the dream. Fortunately if we want to do so we can withhold some of the energy with which we habitually feed this barrier. A simple psychological technique can help enormously in the early stages, when one tiny psychic insight will give you the enthusiasm that will help you through later stages.

Failing to recall dreams is not an omission on your part . . . something you don't do. Not remembering is a positive act. You choose to forget your dreams. By habitually feeling unable to remember dreams, you are actually making a very definite announcement about yourself. Is this announcement any of the following?

I don't really want to know what is going on underneath my conscious mind. I might learn something painful or have to change myself in some way.

I'm not really deep enough for this sort of stuff. I'm more the practical type. Let's be normal . . . after all.

There's a lot of bizarre sex and violence in my dreams. I really had better leave such things alone. What would people say, and how could I speak about what happens in them without blushing?

I must remain in control of my life. I like myself the way I am, thank you very much, and I'll change myself in the way I want when I'm good and ready, without getting carried away by dreams.

I think I'll sleep forever. The thought of the day I'm about to be hurled into makes me shut off my brain completely.

I must remember my dreams! I've just read a book about it, and I'd like to impress people with how well informed I am on the subject.

The way to free yourself from such blocks that arise in your thought patterns is simply to notice them. The rest follows automatically. You will soon develop a willingness to remember what you have dreamed.

The land of dreams

Logic has no place in the fluid dream world though there are consistent patterns. As you wander around dream world, the things you see are images you are creating yourself. The feelings coming toward you from the dream surroundings are just as much you as you are! The landscape is created out of your awareness. Consequently, though things appear outside you (in the dream) you also feel yourself to be present in the things you are perceiving. You are here as well as there. The result is a kind of back to front, can't-tell-the-difference-between coming-or-going-world.

I'm sure you know the dream where a bell rings at the end of a dream saga which seems to have been building logically up to this bell-ringing finale for hours. And yet you know full well that the bell was actually someone downstairs dropping a pan, and the sound was only added to your dream totally without warning at the end. So how did the dream build up so logically to an ending that was completely unforseeable?

In dreams, time starts at the end and works backwards, and at the same time starts at the beginning and goes forwards to meet itself in the middle!

Feelings in dreams start outside you and come inwards towards you, often rushing towards you as if they were something else other than you.

Things you say in dreams are what you are supposed to hear being said to you. Things you hear, are actually issuing from you.

It's a potential minefield for interpretations when you wake up, so beware of the obvious! And don't take to heart well meaning interpretations from other people. They will only confuse the situation.

The old technique of requesting a dream sincerely in response to a clear and humble question in your heart is the best approach to dreaming. When your dream comes in this way you will naturally understand it, and reflect sensitively and in your own way on any hazy bits until a clear understanding fills your heart.

Other major questions
Ask yourself: who is dreaming the dream? It is quite possible to say to yourself in your dream, 'Oh it's only a dream,' and carry on still in the thick of the action of the same dream! Your identity in dream-world is nowhere near as clear cut as it is in everyday life. It peels back like the layers of an onion. You can wake up, and then wake up yet again. Something called 'you' is controlling the dream, and that's fine as long as the you that is controlling the dream fits with the you of real life. But when it wants to, it literally wakes you up in the dream . . . and suddenly you become two yous! You and you plus . . . a brand new being you were formerly unaware of takes control of the dream. So you cannot approach dream experience only with logic.

This 'waking up' in a dream begs a further revealing question: Is it possible to 'fall asleep' in a dream? Could you actually be dreaming and then, in your dream, fall asleep into an even deeper consciousness? Well, yes it *is* entirely possible, it is the richest source of psychic understanding I know. It is by scientific definition a state called '*unconscious* dreamless sleep' because we are used to visual dream imagery as being the only alternative to nothing at all. It is very much like the sun dominance situation that prevails in the outer world. In that case, it's a matter of sun or nothing. In this, it is moon or nothing.

The bright visual dreams of the early morning, and, for those who choose to remember them, dreams of night, have great value. But for true psychic insight you have to try to achieve the impossible state of being conscious of the dream life that takes place when you fall asleep from your visual dreams! This is probably too much to believe for many of us. The idea that you should try to know something moving within you even in your 'unconscious' dreamless sleep phases seems contradictory to all reason. How does it get in touch, if I am fast asleep and it does not speak the picture language of a dream?

Before I answer that question, may I point out that the faith element operates here more than anywhere. I am directing you to look for activity of an unknown kind in an apparently unpromising and empty place. Be assured that the simple act of doing this will help you most to get a result. The energies present in dreamless sleep communicate via what I can only describe as a kind of inner sound. Words more meaningful than our words, in a language that can't be described as verbal but still communicates. If a human could speak this language every time they said anything, the actual thing would appear from their mouth, not a word saying the thing. From this place within deep sleep comes this 'sound' of a deep knowing. This knowing is like the feeling of the stars on a clear night. Psychic insights given in this way can be brought back to waking consciousness just as can the understandings of the visions of ordinary dream life. Fragments of this deep world can be made part of waking life if our attitude is correct, and we have a little patience. It is vital you try to take what you can from this world and make it your own in your waking world. You will have to proceed very slowly in this. It is not the kind of once a week 'Oh-look-what-I've-learned-today' sort of learning at all. Be open to it and patient and you will receive some very real illumination from your non-dreams!

If you find this talk about dreamless sleep dreaming incomprehensible, do read it again and make a few investigations over the days and weeks for yourself. Once your patience is rewarded, you will add a new dimension to your potential for psychic insight.

Understanding 'real' dreams

For now, back to some of the ways of real dreams, if I can call them that. These are much more under your control, and simply waiting to be delved into and understood. The first thing you have to decide after a dream that arrived unasked for is whether it is worth interpreting. There are many apparently meaningful dreams that in no way have the depth they might appear to have. To decide whether a dream is simply a random blast of symbol-code that only a skilled Jungian therapist could crack after three years in depth analysis, or whether it is something personal, needing only tender reflection to release its secret, is quite easy. Do you remember in the last chapter how I pointed out the existence of a lower 'creature' that made up the systems of your trunk and abdomen?

This creature has no rational brain of its own, and no senses with which to communicate to the outside world. However it does communicate with the other creatures making up the body. One of its main communications with the head is through dreams. Being non-rational, like a child, it makes itself felt with considerable force, and speaks a symbolic language of pictures. You should check first whether the images that arise in your dreams are in fact symbolic messages from various parts of your body. From my experience, this is likely. Wondering about the significance of a huge snake, and a pillar of flame, could keep you agonizing for weeks. Sensitivity to the possibility that you are getting a message from your intestines that they are over active (snake), and from your circulation that you have too many blankets on and are too hot (flame), could save you some wondering!

The individual parts of the body can be quite specific in their messages, and if you wake up and immediately check through the images you have been visited with, you can often find a feeling in the relevant part. The most likely time for these dreams is just before you wake up. Then you will often get encoded messages particularly from a part of your body that is not as it should be, either temporarily or perhaps chronically. But this is not a substitute for medical advice of course.

If your dream survives this first, thoroughly check for hidden symbols of the body, the chances are that you have a meaningful little sequence of events and characters in your head waiting for some explanation to occur to you. It is important to realize that you must do this interpretation for yourself. As for opinions on details, by all means, but never accept wholesale an opinion from another person. Never. One or two points might be clarified, but the interpretation, which is the final simple thing that you carry back into the real world and apply, this must always be yours . . . no matter how long it takes you to arrive at it. The interpretation of a dream or a recurring dream may take years to arise in extreme cases, but if you take responsibility for your dream, it will always reveal its secret to you in the end . . . and usually at exactly the right time.

Remember this: your dream is your creation and looks to you as its creator! The process of getting to know it from now on is basically to ask questions. Relate to this dream as if it were a person whom you suddenly found in your garden! You must find out what it wants and then be rid of it! Most dreams have got something to say to you; that is their purpose.

Things to do with dreams

There is usually an element of conflict in a meaningful dream. You must identify what is opposing what. When you have done so, you can carry the dream on in your mind in a way I will explain later, and lead it to an imaginary, but for you, acceptable ending. That is one way of getting rid of it.

If it isn't conflict, then there is usually something unresolved in a dream. Some situation that looked as if it were going to happen but didn't. Often a predictable course of events is interrupted unexpectedly and most likely you wake up with an incomplete feeling, wondering what was going to happen next. Think back as clearly as you can, to what it was you were expecting to happen had your dream not been interrupted. When you are clear about this, recall what it was that stopped it from happening, made the expected outcome impossible. The answer is in there somewhere, but you may have to strain your memory to find out. You may find a feeling like the one you get when you are wondering where you left some misplaced item. Persevere for a few minutes, and it will come to you. If you just let it slide, the meaning will probably be lost.

You are responsible for your dream creation, and you are going to ask it questions. Here, in no deliberate order of priority are some questions to ask. Read through and see if any one or two strike home in some way. Remember, the dream has spoken to you.

What are you saying to me about my sexual feelings?

What are you saying to me about when I was a child?

What are you telling me about how I feel about money?

What are you saying about my attitude towards my mother? And my father?

Are you trying to tell me about my ways of making decisions and choices? Or how I avoid making choices?

What possibilities about my future are you pointing to?

Are you talking to me about anything political? Do world events' feature in some way?

Are you telling me about a need I have to heal myself in some way?

Are you telling me about a personality trait I have?

There are, of course, many more relevant questions you might ask. But remember, you are only looking for a question or two that strike a note. You don't have to work through in an orderly way, or remember the questions! Here are a few more:

What are you telling me about my past? Either my past situation, or past feelings I used to hold?

Are you pointing to an attitude I hold about something?

Are you referring to a mistake I keep making?

Are you hinting at something I'm afraid of?

Are you telling me about the possibilities of my life in the future?

Is there some change that I need to make?

Are you telling me about my inability to love someone?

Am I blaming someone else?

Most of these questions you will be asking yourself, wide awake, about a dream you have already had. However, if you have taken any of them to heart, you will soon find yourself actually asking questions in your dreams. You will address the major characters or things. The people who appear in your dream are worth interrogating! Even if you recognize them, ask them openly what they are doing there, and get a dialogue going. If you can't remember to do it in the dream, don't worry. Simply reflect on what you can remember and try out a few questions in your imagination.

Who are you?

What are you?

What are you doing in my dream?

Why are you behaving in this way in my dream?

Are you trying to tell me something?

What do you think about x . . . (some event that has occurred in the dream)?

Why has x . . . (an event from the dream) . . . happened?

What do you want from me, or want me to do?

What questions would you ask me, if this dialogue were the other way round?

How do you feel about all my questions to you?

What is your gift to me?

What should I ask you?

Is what you are saying true?

Why do I need this dream?

How am I acting in this dream?

Who are my enemies?

What actions are you suggesting I consider?

What choice will I make as a result of talking to you?

Who is my friend?

Why am I afraid/ happy at seeing you?

If you manage to get an answer in the dream, use your memory very carefully the moment you wake up! The key information you are looking for is not so much what is said in answer to your question (though this is a good start if it is all you can come up with at first). What counts is what you say before you ask your question. And also . . . what you then say after the answer is given!

In the backwards world of dreams the answer arrives before the question, so it is true to say that what you speak before asking your question is the answer, or at least a relevant point for learning something. And what you say after you have heard the answer is in fact the seeds of a very valid question! I have found the above to be true, and many apparently meaningless statements made at these times have proved to be quite revealing after a little reflection. The fact that they may at first sight seem to be nonsense is an advantage.

Most of us are in the habit of looking to our interpretations of dreams to prove to ourselves how clever we are, and are unconsciously looking out to hear something we already know. Words spoken at the points I have mentioned are usually surprising and significant.

EXERCISE: *Revisiting a dream*

As I said earlier, it is quite possible to get back into a dream to continue it to a conclusion if this wasn't reached before interruption, or perhaps to resolve some conflict between elements in a dream. There are two techniques:

Technique one
Simply summon as much of the dream as possible into your memory and then go to sleep. Follow on dreams like this are possible. The space between the first dream and the sequel, is unimportant. Anything from a minute to a year. As long as you have made an effort to remember as much as you can, and you fall asleep with a sincere *intention* to resolve the elements of the dream, you will have success.

Technique two
This method requires some silence and a period set aside for deliberate imagining and daydreaming.

1 *Lie down or get comfortable.*

2 *You are now going to mentally divide yourself in half! While awake, one half is going to look back dreamily in your mind's eye at what it can remember of the dream, to re-live it, and the other half is going to stay observing and separate and jump into the action when it wants to and redirect things the way it chooses. Remember your dream as it was.*

3 *Now drop in at some point and question the participants. Their answers will be quite audible in one or other of your 'halves'. It all happens quite naturally.*

As for changing the action, once you have jumped in, you will be surprised by how it all seems to carry on in its own way. Although this re-dreaming may seem to be a rather artificial process, it's amazing how spontaneously the imagination picks up with the energy of the dream, and tends to go its own way whatever your conscious intentions. Sudden new flashes of action take place without being consciously willed by you. If your intention is to resolve conflicts, you will succeed in some unexpected ways. Simply let your imagination wander and guide the dream gently but firmly towards a happy conclusion.

With apparently unfinished dreams, all you have to do is carry the action on after the point when it finished the first time, to a point in your imagination where you feel all right about it. Once again, expect the unexpected. All sorts of possibilities are possible here, depending on how relaxed you feel, how deep your imagination, and many other factors. Let the dialogue and action wander as far as it likes, before you impose the solution or outcome you have in mind. Make sure you resolve it though ... it's easy to start up a daydream that simply continues the unresolved feeling, wandering off into a haze!

It is worth noting that you can continue a dream in two ways:

You can run it on past the end, where it stopped.

You can run it back before the beginning where it started.

If it helps, visualize the situation out of which the dream arose. Who or what was doing what. And where?! And to whom? And with whom? Before the beginning is a very fruitful place for insight.

4 *When you have finished your reverie, be sure you return yourself firmly to the real world of sense and solid objects.*

As always, do some simple physical thing to 'ground' yourself. For example, clap your hands, make a cup of coffee (caffeine-free perhaps) or brush your teeth. Anything physical will do. Returning to non-mental life is vital. If you are likely to forget this, I don't recommend you to do the above exercise at all. You must return to clear-cut, awareness and forget your daydream completely now.

8
TRADITIONAL
PSYCHIC TECHNIQUES

Until now we have been concerned with getting in touch with a deep psychic awareness or insight. I think we have now progressed sufficiently to enable you to have a taste of a less stable form of psychic knowledge. In this chapter we are going to come to grips with the 'time based' clairvoyance mentioned way back in Chapter Three. Probably this is the area of psychic growth that first caught your imagination. It is definitely the most sensational: it includes predicting the future, knowing the past, hearing voices, finding lost objects, knowing what people are thinking, even getting in touch with people who are no longer living. Each of these activities has its own name, such as clairvoyance (literally seeing light), psychometry (getting impressions from an object), clairaudience (hearing things), scrying (crystal ball reading), trance mediumship, spirit mediumship (where spirits speak through the medium), physical mediumship (making things arrive out of nowhere) and even exorcism.

Altogether, this is potentially a very sticky subject, and you had best know this from the start. So let me say once and for all (or I will have to keep repeating it after everything I write) your attempts at practising the techniques I am about to tell you will only be to your benefit if they come third on your list of priorities! Let me explain:

Your first priority is your daily material life; you must keep this in order and happy.

Second, comes the broader searching after clairvoyant insight that we have been pursuing so far; this keeps you in harmony with the natural psychic forces in the world around you, and is always unfolding and young.

Third (and well down on the list in my opinion) is this practising of specific man-made psychic tasks, such as fortune telling, or doing psychic reading. These are distinctly ego inflating activities with a momentum of their own. They do not necessarily keep you in touch with either the solid world of good sense, or the spiritual rhythms of broader insight.

You must feel firmly grounded in your daily world, and firmly grounded in your moral feelings (see Chapter Four again) for psychic activities such as these to work happily for you. There is no need to feel worried about it; simply be aware of the potential for deluding yourself, and go easily, stopping if you feel the slightest mental or physical discomfort. If you have worked this far into the book you will definitely broaden your psychic understanding quite considerably by looking into these lesser, more earthbound, psychic activities.

Basically, what you are getting into here is fortune telling. Try to dignify it as you will, this is the situation. There are popular magazines devoted to the subject of psychism, and in their classified pages are lists of practising psychics offering their services. These people use their psychic abilities to help and advise others on how to get the best out of their daily life.

The psychic practitioner uses whatever method they are skilled in — anything from Rune-Stones to Astrology — to help their client to gain some advantage in their daily life. This is a perfectly good use of potential, both the psychic's and the client's, but it must be firmly realized that that is what is going on. When you turn to your clairvoyant powers to give some direct advantage in the future, or the past, the correct label is fortune telling. Be quite clear about this. Don't confuse it with any deeper spiritual feelings you might have had to date.

To begin with I will take your through one of the most picturesque and quaint psychic practices going . . . tea-leaf reading. It is the best subject for sharpening your psychic wits on that I know. Traditionally it is a light-hearted and easygoing pursuit, yet it contains the essence of all methods of fortune telling. It is distinctly down-to-earth, requiring as it does cups, saucers and sloppy tea leaves. All this is a tremendous asset. There's nothing worse than a 'heavy' atmosphere for deadening budding psychic abilities. When the pressure is on most of us freeze over.

It is a fact that nobody is going to take the slightest long-term notice of your first tea-leaf readings, and at the beginning that is just how you want it! If psychic readings were one hundred per cent correct we'd all be rich, and the world would be a different place, so accept from the first moment of your fortune telling that you are going to say some things that are completely wrong! This is best done over a quick cup of tea, rather than in any way ceremoniously. In such circumstances the odds are in your favour. Clients will be willing to see success in any prediction you make; and this will give you confidence. For your part, however, you will have to see it differently. You had best develop a very long memory, particularly for predictions and statements you didn't get right. This is a positive procesTs. When you get going you will soon be making more hits than you expected. The excitement generated is immense. Remembering errors keeps your excitement down to a manageable level, and causes you to practise and control your psychic powers.

Keeping records

Anyone who is about to start experimenting with psychic observations and predictions, ought to keep a record of what they have said. A personal psychic journal. List your predictions and statements, dates and times etc. on one side, and on the other side write down what actually happens. This way you can keep a firm check on your accuracy rate, and chart your improvement or deterioration as conditions in your life fluctuate. However, I can't ask you to do this, just as I couldn't ask you to write down your dreams as soon as you wake up. This is the counsel of perfection, and many of us simply don't want to do it, and won't. If you have the sort of a mind that *can* regularly keep records, do keep a journal. Or, if you feel the enthusiasm to keep records later in your experience, then start halfway in by all means. But if you don't want to write, don't. Rely instead on your own mental checks on yourself to chart progress.

Sooner or later you will learn that, as with all activities, psychic ability improves with practice and self-observation. As for the possibility of self-delusion, it is a self-regulating thing. If you are sincere about what you are doing and why you are doing it, your delusion will be removed automatically by some 'lesson-teaching' experience that crops up in your daily life. Some say this is your 'Guardian Angel' at work!

Doing a psychic reading — even 'tasseomancy' (tea leaf reading) — takes courage. You never can be sure what you are going to say. You may even say nothing at all! Even so, the sheer humility of tea-leaves is ideal for a beginner. You are with a friend, and you are under no real pressure to come up with the goods! So give it a try. Invite your friends round for a cup of the finest Darjeeling, or whatever and proceed as follows.

Tea leaf reading

As with all fortune telling techniques, the essential actions you have to do are very little, and they are not strictly defined. You do not have to buy a book by the world's most expert reader of tea leaves and faithfully copy the technique. This wouldn't help you at all. It is largely the *attitude* of the person doing the reading that produces a psychic result, not what they do.

The following is all that is needed:

1 *Make a cup of tea. Don't strain it as you pour it out (obviously, no tea-bags).*

2 *Drink the tea, then swill the dregs around in the bottom of the cup.*

3 *Turn the cup over, place it lip downwards in the saucer and let the dregs drain out.*

4 *Pick up the cup, and peer into it at the patterns the leaves make as they stick to the inside.*

5 *Get your child-like visual imagination going. Switch mentally into visual mode, as you practised in earlier chapters.*

These are no longer tea-leaves, they are images of things. As you look at them you must want some picture or object to form out of the patterns.

6 *The following may sound strange, but it's true. You should suddenly feel very lonely at this point.*

From being with your friend in the real world, simply chatting, you must now close yourself off *completely* to everything around you, except these few forms in the bottom of the cup. You will feel a kind of loneliness. You are supposed to do so; that is how it happens.

7 *As you look at the shapes, it is as if you are pushing something in your whole body upwards out of the top of your head.*

This is not a tensing up of muscles, it is an inner feeling as if you are trying to see with everything you have, but out of a space just above the top of your head. You make an inner psychic movement upwards.

8 *Your eyes will feel as if they want to look upwards, but let them stay gently downwards, looking at the leaves.*

They may lose focus as you increase your feeling upwards. That is fine, it helps blur the edges of the leaves and makes them less like what they are and more like what you want to turn them into (things). Don't gaze rigidly. Glance about the inside of the cup, and try to see what you can. This is the middle, waiting, hopeful stage. Hold this upward force and wait.

9 *The final stage comes as a relief. As you hold your awareness — pushing it upwards — suddenly, from around your stomach region, an awareness, a knowing slots in, inwards.*

It is as if it fills a space created in you by pushing your awareness upwards. (Remember it is in no way a PHYSICAL or tense pushing upwards. It is psychic.) Suddenly, a clear object will become visible in your mind, in the dark patterns of the leaves, and it will bring with it a distinct urge to speak.

Often, you can be waiting an uncomfortably long time for that clear inward stomach feeling, and the visual resolution that follows immediately. There will be an awful temptation to let yourself off the hook, and to say absolutely anything, just to be sure that you don't look foolish.

Wait, if you can, and have faith. This always helps. While you are waiting, thoughts, ideas and words will come crowding into your mind, each seemingly exactly the right one for you to put forward to make the best effect. Try to resist and filter them out carefully. Always go for the one that comes out of the inward-moving lower stomach feeling. Then you can let go of your upward lifting out-of-the-top-of-your-head effort. It is time to speak!

Talking about it
Obviously you will do a lot of speaking if you read fortunes. But our powers of speech must be used carefully. There is a clear connection in occult tradition, between the vocal forces and the energies of regeneration. The larynx and the womb are closely related. Give it some thought, and so, proceed with respect for the words you are giving birth to!

Psychic realities don't store in the memory. They are created anew each time, so you should hope to find an element of surprise in what you say to your friend or client. If what you say sounds cool

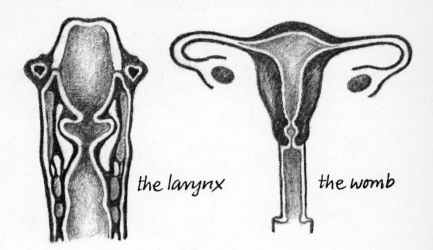

the larynx   the womb

and easy, there is a fair chance that you are waffling. Every psychic statement has to be fresh as if it were being said for the first time, every time. There is an effort involved in this activity of generating original, psychically inspired material, that you can feel very clearly. You will know when you have spoken from an inspired place within you. It wells up from underneath.

All experienced psychics know the effort of letting themselves be open to inspired information for a long time, and are careful not to overdo it. It takes intense concentration, and can be draining. Be aware of this. Many people give up time-based clairvoyance for precisely this reason. To do it well requires effort, and unlike the higher clairvoyant investigations which always brings renewal, fortune telling can seem at times to deplete your mental energies. You may feel worn out even after reading just one tea cup properly!

However, now you have experienced that inspired feeling the time has come to open your mouth and speak. Here is a two-part process to get you started:

If the pattern that arose up in you looks like a fish for example, simply say, 'I can see a fish.' Get it off your chest. That's the first bit and it couldn't be simpler.

Now you are going to make a further, deeper statement. You will find this statement in your stomach. It is attached in some way to the image you have seen in your head, but it is from around your stomach that you will draw it up. This second comment will be more complex, and will arise out of the first. It could be something like: 'You are going fishing', or 'You are keen on aquariums.'

These two statements will do fine, but the chances are that your second statement will be much less directly connected with the image. Expect more unlikely statements to arise in you. Seeing the fish could lead to something like: 'What a big one! I think you could have been telling some whoppers lately!' or, less provocatively, 'I think you're about to land something.' Do you get the idea?

To start off with, simply limit yourself to two such statements. One simple declaration of what has appeared, and another, broader, opening out, wandering expression of a general nature, inspired by your vision in the cup.

Let's take another example. Say you can see a saw, but a saw seems so unlikely, so dull. There is no apparent connection between your client (perhaps a slightly built ballerina!) and the mighty blade that appears to you. Never mind. Don't reject this strongly felt image simply because it doesn't seem to make any sense. You won't know for sure what makes sense or not, until you make your second statement out loud. Have courage and say: 'I can see a saw', or words to that effect. 'A great big, rusty, agricultural-strength, heavy-duty saw.'

You may then suddenly find yourself going on to say, 'Something is being cut in half, some sharing is taking place.' It could well turn out that your ballerina's parents are separating and dividing up some land . . . a farm? Do you see how it works? Insights like this definitely do occur.

Sometimes, the image you have moves, fades or dribbles as you look at it. For example, the shape of a foot may suddenly dissolve. Say something like, 'I see a foot', then, 'But now I don't. I think you might be about to lose a shoe or something.' It may seem weird and banal written down like this, but wait until you try it and your prediction turns out to be true! Remember though, keep it light-hearted and predict only for about the next week or so. Reading tea-leaves is not a good opportunity for making profound statements about people's destinies, especially if they haven't asked you to do so. So, any feelings of 'heaviness' should be kept exclusively to yourself as it probably arises from your psychic efforts at lifting your awareness above your head! Please resist any temptation to inflict dire statements about the future on your happy client. This inclination is normal, but it must be resisted.

Often, it is only at the last possible second that the feeling that makes you talk comes, and an image drops into place. If things get desperate, you may have to break off and chat casually for a few seconds, then look again into the cup. Probably, you will then see something.

Some last words about talking. Get used to starting a sentence, and having no idea how it is going to finish. In this psychic tea-cup reading, feel free to start speaking with only a picture in your mind's eye, and not the slightest idea of what will follow after your first few words. The opening words will create a momentum of their own, and will help to draw up suitable statements from the correct lower part of your body — the stomach.

Finally, be well aware of the following. It applies as much to everyday talking as it does to psychic speech. As you speak, as well as the stream of sounds, words and meaning that flow outwards from you towards the person you are talking to, there exists another, balancing stream of energy. This moves backwards and into you. It is a distinct stream of feeling, that you can consciously pursue deep into yourself. It starts like your words, in and around your throat and mouth area, but as you talk, it moves backwards, then upwards and downwards . . . not outwards into the world. Whatever you say will affect you via this stream, as much if not more than it affects the people you talk to. It carries inwards the essence, good, bad or indifferent of whatever you choose to say.

Develop your sensitivity to this mirror image of your talking. It should always feel fresh. If it feels negative or uncomfortable, the chances are you are saying things that are not helping your client (or you!). The solution is simply to notice what you are feeling and doing, and let adjustments arise in their own time. This backwards and inwards feeling that you create with every word you speak aloud is a wonderful barometer for the sincerity of your psychic observations. When you make a good prediction, it somehow flows from inside of you, in a way that tells you that you have said exactly the right thing.

Listening

Now I'm going to tell you about the other vital part of good fortune telling . . . listening.

The main thing you are going to get from your listening at first is confidence. If you've taken your courage, and their cup, in your hands and made statements of a psychic nature as directed above, it is very likely indeed that the response you get will surprise you. If you have made the slightest attempts at psychic development along the lines I have shown throughout this book, you will be pretty certain to say something revealing or in some way clairvoyant.

Your client will then become much more attentive to you. Before your reading you may have been chatting, exchanging views quite amiably, but now that you have begun to speak from your psychic perspective, you will find the mood of the exchange between you and your client is much more focused on you, and what you have to contribute.

When you stop to let the other person speak you will find their attitude towards you quite different from usual. They will attach great weight to what you have said, and it will be evident that they have been touched in some way. This is surprising the first time it happens, so be ready. They will want to know more from you.

Many people never get beyond this point. As soon as their client speaks to them with the respect due to someone who has made a helpful psychic observation, they put all their energies into listening to their client's comments in search of whatever clues, hints and giveaways they can find. The hope of scoring another impressive bull's-eye is irresistible and all their listening is unconsciously directed to this end.

Many psychics also do this. They intersperse one, or two at the most, psychic insights with a lot of conjecture and deductions that they have been keenly observing in their client's responses. The animating effect on the atmosphere of the first psychic direct hit, gets everyone so excited that the client forgets natural defences and blurts out whatever comes into their head, quite unaware of what they have said. A bit of shrewd guesswork on the part of an enthusiastic reader can maintain the client's befuddled state for some time. Then the reader simply plays back a few sentences later what the clients themselves have already stated or implied!

Be ready for this. Expect to be treated with a new respect when you hear your client's reactions to your first observations. They may well try to mask it in a joke or a slightly hollow laugh, but you will be able to feel the underlying 'touched' feeling that they have experienced. The following is a good technique to proceed with.

For listening purposes, you are going to have to divide yourself in two (as you did in interpreting your dreams). One half of you is going to be the authority that your psychic insight naturally bestows on you. And the other half has to be completely humble and believing whatever your client might say to you. Let me clarify.

If you are responding as best you can to psychic perceptions felt within you, I hope you have not hesitated to speak them. If your client has asked for your opinion and is aware you are developing psychically, you must speak out. In the early stages, when doing readings for people you know, you will often have to step completely out of the normal bounds of your relationship with them. For instance, in this leaf-reading situation, you may be light-heartedly talking to a friend you have known for years. Then, after a few minutes of the reading you could be almost scolding them for not respecting the wishes of their parents enough, or advising them in no uncertain terms to take better care of their health. You would not offer either pieces of advice to them in your usual relationship. In fact, you may not even realize that you have suddenly changed your role, as it usually appears in the mind of the listener, rather than through any change of tone or any conscious thing that you might do. So, be clear and authoritative — as long as you have the consent of your client and it is obvious that they are requesting psychic news from you. Give them your psychic observations and stand by them.

You must also listen with absolute authority, but what you have said, you have said. Do not let your client talk you out of anything, or request you to agree to any changes of meaning. Don't let what you have said become a subject for negotiation. So much for the authoritative side.

Now for the other half, the humble side. It is perfectly possible to be both utterly authoritative and humble at the same time. What you are being so authoritative about is something that (hopefully) came to you in a sincere psychic way and which you have merely presented. It is *not* an opinion of yours that you have to defend. A sincere psychic insight has a life of its own. All you are doing by being firm is protecting it, and letting it exist for long enough to enter into your client's awareness. Do not try to disarm them, or in any way contradict their opinions. This is your humble bit. No matter what a person says to you, listen with cool detachment. Do not hurl back opinions of your own. Neither verbally, nor mentally. Hurling opinions against each other would be very destructive to your psychic ability.

It is worth noting that opinion hurling is one of the commonest activities of the day. Most 'normal' conversation is little more than this. One person speaks, and the other one, instead of opening up and listening, is busily lining up their opinions ready for the moment when they get a chance to hurl opinions of their own back! Very little actual listening takes place. Notice it for yourself. Every few words that are spoken to you, you will find a response stirring inside your head. It's as if a little voice in you is constantly commenting, 'Yes, that's right,' 'Oh no! you can't say that,' or

'Well, I wouldn't quite put it like that,' or, 'Rubbish! How dare you suggest such a thing.' This inner clamour is quite deafening, and leaves you with very little energy to tune in to the deeper feelings that lie behind what the other person is saying. So, when listening to your client, try to silence this tendency in yourself. If you feel a reaction arising against something they are saying, *leave it alone*. You have had your say, now listen humbly and refrain from comment! It is not easy but it is essential to cultivate from the very first tea-leaf reading.

One last point. Whatever you have to do or say to find an optimistic note, don't ever forget to close the session with firm good news. It is your responsibility to return the conversation to normal, positive and happy realms. With tea-leaf readings it shouldn't be hard to laugh the whole thing off if necessary. Tell a joke, sing a song or break out the vodka. But *do* bring your client back into the real, everyday world, and on a high note.

Psychometry

Psychometry literally means soul-measuring. A 'psychometric reading' is nothing more than picking up or touching an object and seeing what impressions come into your mind. It is sometimes referred to as object reading. As you will readily appreciate, in terms of actual technique, there is even less to it than reading tea-leaves. About the only definite tradition that has grown up around this method is that of placing the object you are going to read on your forehead. This allegedly helps you get the 'vibrations' from the object closer to your 'third eye'. Certainly, it works for me, and I don't hesitate to place an object near my forehead if I want to read it, but whether or not this is anything to do with third eyes or vibrations I seriously question. It feels right, so I do it, and this is a procedure I recommend.

The traditional explanation is that matter is able to contain and record vibrations, and some materials hold these vibrations better than others. For this reason, many psychics can only read old precious objects such as gold or silver jewellery. Other sensitives can read paper objects or even plastic ones. That says very little for the infallible truth of the stored vibrations theory! I don't think the theories need concern you. If you have a talent for it you will get results. It doesn't seem to matter what you do, what part of your body you 'read' the object with, or in fact what the object is, or is made of. As ever, what does matter is the state of mind of you, the reader.

Before I discuss psychometry further I would add a word or two about individual psychic talents. You are about to consider trying a second traditional psychic technique. Please do not expect to be successful in all techniques. Psychic development at this level is very much a search for the one or perhaps two methods that are best for you. A person who has an easy affinity with tea-leaf reading may find the following psychometry exercise abstract and confusing. Similarly, a crystal ball may have instant appeal to some, who then try clairaudience or direct clairvoyant readings and get absolutely nothing. How you find the technique that suits you is for you and you alone to discover. Just try a few and see what happens. But remember, always keep your mind open. You may have hidden talents that will not show themselves until your psychic development has advanced a little further. This is very common. What's more, your particular talent, once you realize what it is, will probably turn out to be something you have been doing quite unconsciously since childhood. So look back into your earliest memories and see if anything there gives you a clue as to your best area for psychic ability. We all have some psychic talent hidden away.

Psychometry is a very gentle technique, and requires a considerable degree of sensitivity, at least I find it so. Compared to tea-leaf reading, you need to be more introspective and must start in a quieter environment. There is less to concentrate on visually, and I find it requires a still awareness to get results. Also, you are unlikely to start doing it casually over a cup of tea with a friend. You will probably want to practise it alone first, and only then try it out on someone else. This initial working alone makes psychometry a very good starting point for developing sensitivity that will give you a firm psychic base to build on. You must keep a clear perspective on your results though, note-taking where necessary, to keep your impressions, correct and false, in perspective. Then encouraged by your successes you can take your new found skill out into the world, and present it in the lighthearted social 'tea-cup-reading' situation.

Object reading deals usually with the past. There have been cases of archaeological psychometry where sensitives have put together detailed, and later verified, pictures of history from one fragment of a pot. Your first efforts will probably be much more vague and personal!

Experience suggests that psychometry will not produce sharp, clear cut pictures as if watching some kind of television. You will be trying to evaluate changing, varying impressions and fleeting, mobile pictures, and the transition of one into the other. Obviously, you will need the quietest possible background. If your head is full of your own thoughts, you will not be able to sort out what is yours and what belongs to the object you are reading. This brings us to the business of relaxation.

EXERCISE: *Simply relax*

There are many different methods of relaxation, to suit the needs of different personalities. So the relaxed state so essential to psychometry can be acquired by anyone. I am going to give you two relaxation techniques here, and you may like to try others of your own.

Technique one
Use this visualization technique as you sit for psychometry; really try to experience it in your mind. It will help if, at first, you practise this in a quiet, comfortable place where you are not likely to be disturbed.

1 *Imagine that it is a warm summer's afternoon and you are reclining comfortably in a peaceful garden. You are on holiday, and there is nothing that you have to do. Everything is secure and you feel quiet and carefree. You can hear birds singing in the distance and, and a bee drones lazily by.*

2 *You begin to drowse. Hold that drowsing moment.*

You can achieve this carefree drowsing state quite easily, simply by using your powers of fantasy.

Technique two
Here is my second technique of relaxing; some consider it eccentric, but it works.

1 *Get a seashell of the kind in which, when you put it to your ear, you can hear the sound of sea.*

2 *Sit yourself comfortably down in a quiet place, and make the following clear decision to yourself: I have come to this place with my shell for no other reason than to sit and listen to the sea for five minutes. I am not here to think about anything else. As soon as I do notice myself thinking, I will return to the sound of my shell.*

Set this clearly as your goal, but be prepared to have a wandering mind, and forgive yourself every time you slip. Concentrate as best you can for the odd two or three seconds at a time in your five minute session. Don't get frustrated or anxious at your initial inability to concentrate, or you'll get more and more wound up instead of more and more relaxed! It does take time and practice to achieve this.

3 *Just sit and listen to the sound of the sea in your shell.*

Concentrate and you will be surprised how soothing the sound becomes and the gentle 'shushing' tone provides a constant and pleasant reference point to return your wandering mind to. Relax and drift into it as far as you like. There is psychic inspiration within it. If you do the above as often as possible you will feel real benefit.

EXERCISE: *Private practice*

Now an exercise that will show you clearly the inner details of psychic perception involved. You will need an envelope large enough to hold a standard-size photograph, and your family album or an assortment of photographs.

1 *Look through the album and take out an assorted selection of family, friends, acquaintances, old lovers etc! Choose people who you know quite well, not signed photos of celebrities! Also, choose photographs that are all roughly the same size.*

2 *Put the photos in a box, give it a gentle shake. Then, with closed eyes, select one at random and put it into the envelope. Be sure you have no idea who it is a picture of, either from the shape of it or its feel or any other possible give-away. If you like, do this at night in quiet darkness. It will help to relax your mind.*

3 *Keeping the envelope containing the selected photo close to you, retire to some quiet place. There, light a candle (in a safe holder) and put the envelope on the table next to the candle.*

4 *Now sit and become as still as you possibly can. Thoughts will pass through your mind as ever.*

Simply acknowledge them and let them go. They *will* fade. Then, suddenly, one quite ordinary impression will stand out. You will know quite easily when this happens. Say, for example, you have a stream of thoughts going through your mind and suddenly you find you have the distinct impression of a greenhouse. 'What,' you will probably say to yourself, 'is this greenhouse doing here? It means nothing to me. I have no greenhouse. I don't even know anyone who has a greenhouse!' You will feel an urge to pass on and wait for more significant or dramatic impressions. Stop! Stay right where you are. Always trust your first impressions. Greenhouse is what you have got, so greenhouse it is. In psychometry, first impressions must be seized immediately.

6 *Now pick up your envelope and turn it over in your hands smoothly. Hold it as you will. Put it to your head if you like.*

You should feel some new impression entering the stream of your thoughts. It could be a picture as before, or it could be simply a feeling — say a feeling of wonder or indecision. It might even be a slight pain, or a particular awareness in some part of your body, a slight consciousness perhaps in your shoulder? Don't wait for a second more 'meaningful' impression.

7 *Note this one firmly. When you have noted that first impression, try for one more.*

Perhaps this time you get a thought about a pair of brown suede shoes and it leads into a mental image of some. So that is what you receive after picking up your envelope. A greenhouse, a feeling of indecision, and a pair of brown suede shoes!

8 *Rise from your session, put on the light but let the candle continue to burn for a while. Now open your envelope. It is a picture of your German penfriend. Someone you haven't seen for years. But he hasn't got a greenhouse! Think about him.*

Suddenly you remember the occasion when you first met. You were at a friends and he walked into where you were and said '*Guten morgen*' so loud it surprised you. It was in the greenhouse. Then it all starts to click. The shoes: he always wore those same brown suede shoes from the moment he arrived to the moment he left. They were his trademark almost. You see them again in your mind's eye, even down to the funny lace holes they had. And again you remember, you never seemed to know what to do with him either.

You were always wondering what to do next and where to take him and if he was having a nice time. That is the feeling of indecision. It was your prevailing mood during his stay.

I hope it is starting to make sense. The above scenario would be typical of the sort of impressions and possibilities you would be working with on a first try at psychometry. It is up to you not to stretch it too far and try to read into things, connections that aren't there. However, you will find yourself able to see some startling connections if you trust yourself to concentrate on the images and impressions that stand out in your mind.

There is plenty of scope for scepticism, I know, and the scientific mind will laugh at your 'results'. Don't be put off. What you are learning in the beginning is an understanding of your psychic process. How the impressions and pictures fit together, and which are relevent and in what way. Obviously, the fact that your German penfriend of long ago had brown shoes with funny lace holes is not a very significant piece of information. But the fact is an exciting insight for you. Even a slight success will generate the enthusiasm to try again. Very soon, you will have the ability to grasp many new insights through this psychic means.

When you demonstrate your new psychometric powers to others, you will have to resign yourself to being misunderstood at first. People simply do not understand how hard it is to be coherent when you are concentrating on inner impressions. Also, the sight of expectant, and probably doubting, faces will put you under considerable pressure, so be ready for some long silences! You must only say what you feel, in the order it arrives. Like your first efforts at tea-leaf reading, this will take courage. Your first readings should be with friends who will be able to confirm the observations you make from the objects they hand you. Don't simply pick up interesting objects that you may see around, and 'read' them. You would have no way of verifying any impressions received; neither could you realistically estimate your own psychometric abilities! So, stay close to home at first. Be happy with your successes, and note any unplaceable impressions. It often happens that what seemed a 'miss' will be discovered to be a hit, after a little reflection and time have passed. Also, you will be amazed how quickly you sensitize yourself to objects, with practice.

When people start bringing things to you to be read, get your ego under control and trust your psychic impressions. In many ways, reading for others is easier than testing yourself. Speak of what you see, as you did when reading the tea-leaves. Only this time, add what you feel. If you are anywhere near the mark — and you should be after a little practice — your clients will encourage you! Try not to get excited, and stay with your impressions rather than theirs.

Crystals

Crystals are a good source of inspiration if you are fascinated by psychometry. The study of crystals is an expanding field and there are many groups interested in it, and books about it are being published.

The crystal specialist will know the 'soul-quality' of each of the different minerals. Hopefully however, you won't yet — and this gap in your knowledge will provide you with a rich opportunity for experiments.

If at all possible, try out different sorts of crystals, and note your inner impressions. Each crystal type has very clear-cut ideas associated with it. Some are male, some are female; some heal, some tend to destroy; some are greedy, some give away; some soothe, others excite. Also, minerals are the oldest form of life. They are ancient beings, with many individual qualities and even a kind of personality.

See what impressions you get with some crystals in the same way as you did with the photograph in the candlelight, in the peace and quiet of a favourite psychic reading place. You will be pleasantly awakened I'm sure. Test your observations afterwards with a person or book on the subject.

9
THE CRYSTAL BALL AND DIRECT CLAIRVOYANCE

The crystal ball is the classic and best known psychic method for predicting the future. The popular idea is of an ancient gypsy who peers into her crystal ball, and sees a tall dark stranger! Most people assume that it is the 'magic' power of the crystal that is the key to the success of the whole thing. This is not so. Crystal ball reading is not dependent on any special properties of the crystal, or of any other substance. If you want to be a crystal ball reader it is quite possible and, as with all psychic phenomena, what will produce results is your sincerity and state of mind.

I realize that it is unlikely that anyone who is reading this will have a crystal ball. They are only sold in magical paraphernalia shops, and a decent sized one is very expensive. However, they are beautiful things, so do get one if you can afford to do so. If such a purchase is beyond your means, there are ways round this.

The secret is not the ball, it's the technique of scrying. This is an inner mental process in many ways similar to looking at the leaf patterns in the bottom of cups, and coming up with images, with the aid of your imagination . . . only when you scry, you don't need any shapes to start your imagination going. You simply see things. And you need a perfectly plain, smooth, featureless darkness as a backdrop against which to see them. Traditionally, a ball of crystal was used. The gypsy stared at it in a certain way (which I will clarify soon), and against the blackness was able to see the contents of her imagination arising as images. It doesn't have to be a piece of crystal. Some talented people do it on their fingernail, and other experienced psychics can do it on any surface they choose, or none at all! So, scrying is a psychic process you are perfectly capable of doing, without gypsy ancestry or a crystal.

Now it's time to add a little 'magic' — it's all very well to know you can do it, but to get meaningful results with scrying, you need all the help you can get.

Your state of mind while reading will need to be calm and focused. The object that is to provide the background for your images (your 'speculum') must be familiar to you and yet mustn't have the sort of associations that inspire stray thoughts. Rather it must go some way towards inducing the right, dreamy psychic frame of mind. Atmosphere and environment play such an important part in this technique. They can make for that tiny bit of extra psychic feel that will carry you forward enthusiastically.

If you can't get a crystal ball for your reading, I will tell you soon how to use a much more available speculum.

Reading the crystal is associated with seeing into the future, and is a good technique for doing more in depth and long-term predictions. But before you start, here is some general information about psychic perception of the future. It will help you do better readings.

As soon as you start talking about 'the future' (something that happens all the time in fortune telling) you are immediately suggesting that the future is a real object. It is not. It doesn't even exist yet. In fact, there may be no such thing as the future! Yet all the effort and concentration of fortune telling goes to suggest that the future is something quite actual, but just a little way further along the road. You only need a quick peep, in the right way, and you'll get a glimpse of it as clear as crystal!

Any higher psychic perception will tell you that this is not the case at all. Only the present is clear cut. The future can go where it will. When looking into the future you are looking toward a vague unformed thing that will not as yet have a sharp outline. And a prediction must inevitably be vague if it is to be in any way true to the future. There has to be an element of ambiguity about your visions of tomorrow.

If you say for example: 'Tomorrow you will get up and put on your red hat,' you are tempting providence to make your client deliberately put on their green hat! Whereas, if you hadn't actually expressed your insight, that tomorrow they would be putting on the red hat (something they probably do regularly without thinking), then it would all have turned out exactly as you saw it, and your prediction would have been correct. So, you have to leave scope for the client to read between the lines for themselves in everything you say about the future.

Obviously, some people, are going to accuse you of hiding behind vague generalities. You will just have to accept this. With clairvoyant readings of all kinds, save specific observations for things of the present, and the past. You can and should be as detailed as you like in these two areas.

Although the nature of the future is vague, rest assured you can see it. If you approach the future accepting that you are looking into something incomplete and ambiguous, you will have a very good chance of seeing that part of it that is formed and available to your psychic sight. Psychic prediction is like that; salient pieces are often missing.

I know a person who went to a psychic and, among other things, was told: 'I see you very soon in a place surrounded by many cats.' Three days later, her boyfriend walked out on her. On her way to the place where she thought she might find him, her car broke down completely. She had to call at a house to telephone for mechanical assistance. The lady who opened the door invited her in to use the phone — and the house was full of cats!

The prediction was right as far as it went, though I know she would have like to have heard about the other slightly more significant events that were about to overtake her. But no, all that was available at the time was cats! And that's how predictions are. So don't ever take responsibility for your predictions. If you see something, say so boldly, but allow your client scope for coming to their own conclusions. It is their future you have seen, not yours.

Alternative speculums

Here then are three ideas for your 'speculum':

You could get a plain glass ball, at least 10 cm (4 in) in diameter. These are not too expensive. I do not recommend buying one secondhand. Get a new one, keep it covered and away from everyone but you. Treat it as if it were precious, private, and extremely fragile.

Alternatively, you could use what is called a magic mirror. This is a concave, jet black glass disc, 10 cm (4 in) or so in diameter. If you have a local clock repairer, you could buy a convex glass clock face, and evenly paint or spray the entire convex side with black enamel paint. Place your mirror on a suitable standing device, such as a block of wood or a piece of velvet. Make and treat your home-made speculum with respect and patience. If you were just to grab the nearest piece of old black card, or some such thing, you would be demonstrating clearly your anxiousness and hurry to get a result. If you invest time in getting your personal psychic tool together in this way, the feel of it will always remind you of your mellow state of mind, and will help the scrying process.

The third speculum is the easiest. Get a small bowl of water, and add to it several drops of black ink. Once again, do carry out simple activity in a spirit of calmness and ceremony. Use a bowl that is plain and unobtrusive, and that gives you some pleasure to see. A small wooden one, that you can reserve only for your scrying practice, would be ideal.

EXERCISE: Scrying

There is a tradition that scrying powers are at their best when the moon is waxing, preferably when it is nearly full. (A waxing moon is one that is nightly growing fuller.) So, you might like to choose such a time for your first practice.

In any event, select a time when you won't be interrupted. This is vital. An hour will do.

1 *Light a candle, and place it behind you so that it doesn't cause a glare on the surface of your speculum. Set the speculum on a plain dark cloth, on a table before you, and seat yourself comfortably. The soft, indirect light of a candle will set the correct mood.*

2 *You are now consciously going to enter a mild trance. This is not difficult. You have done it many times before, without realizing it or calling it a trance.*

It is largely a matter of knowing when these occasions were and then trying on various states of mind until you find the trance feeling you are looking for.

Try the feelings in the following exercises and see if they have a mood in common. This mood will help you to begin your trance.

Simply close your eyes slowly and relax. Concentrate on your breath. Feel it going in . . . and out, rhythmically. Hook your wandering mind to this unstoppable beat. Every time you breathe out simply say, in your mind, the word 'one'. Say it mentally for the duration of the outbreath. That's all there is to it. You may also like to think of the word 'one' not as much as a number as in 1,2,3 etc. but as an expression of 'oneness' or wholeness. You will quickly begin to feel considerably lighter. It is important not to try to breathe in any special way: either faster, deeper, slower, harder, or in any clever fashion. The success of this technique does not depend on changing your oxygen balance or anything like that. It simply keeps you in touch with a natural, gentle rhythm.

Another good area to explore, is the time when you are falling asleep. Try and find out exactly what it is you do when you fall asleep! This is a mind boggling activity full of contradictions, but over the course of a few nights, you can get a feel for it. The process of falling asleep has a sort of a half-and-half state in it, just before you actually sink away into oblivion. (The 'hypnogogic state' it is known as.) It is often the time when you think you are falling, and suddenly you jolt yourself awake, breaking your imaginary fall. Cast your mind back to this time, and see if you can recreate some slight semblance of it. Hopefully you won't achieve the state totally, or you really will be in a deep trance, and you'll be too groggy to do any scrying! Keep one part of you firmly in the real world if you feel yourself susceptible to this state, and don't drift right off.

Try this. Recall a time when you were at your most at ease. Perhaps it was whilst sunbathing one time. Maybe it was when you were a child, and you used to curl up in your home-made den or something. Perhaps you can recall the warm 'snug' feel of such comfortable, protected moments. If you can, use your powers of imagination and fantasy to bring back the images or memories, and induce the feelings in yourself again. One or two images will trigger the sensation. Pretty soon you will be able to recall your trance-starting feelings at will.

3 *Now you are in a suitable state of mind to begin your reading. Start off by practising alone. Look at your speculum with a firm but relaxed gaze. Be prepared to look at it for up to about ten minutes.*

On your first session you may not see a thing even then! Don't continue any longer than 15 minutes at this stage. Wake and shake yourself, put on the lights. (Don't blow out the candle yet. Let it burn for a while . . . then blow or snuff it out gently.)

4 *With a little practice you will experience the following. (Everyone reports these phenomena, with only slight personal variations.) You will be looking at the speculum when suddenly the room, and everything around you, seems to go grey and misty. The speculum stands out, almost luminous from within.*

This is accompanied by visual effects such as shimmering lights, sparks, and flashes coming from in or around the ball. A grey mist will seem to whirl over the surface of the ball and cloud shapes appear, then fade.

Please note: all of this is simply a side effect, the opening stage of your trance. But if you become so excited at this 'happening' that you jolt yourself out of your patiently won relaxed state, that is the end of it! If this does happen to you, never mind, try again, and try not to get so excited!

Psychic sneezing!
To get beyond the above 'fiery visions' stage, you will have to learn to hold yourself in a kind of psychic inner balance. To help get a practical idea of the nature of this inner feeling of poise, take a look at the very physical feeling of being about to sneeze! It may sound crazy, but try this exercise next time you are about to sneeze, there are a lot of parallels in the two situtions.

When you next feel a sneeze coming on, instead of giving yourself up to the sneeze impulse right away, and letting it blast through: instead of as it were rushing out immediately to meet the first hint of a desire to sneeze, remain unmoved. Stay where you are, and watch the sneeze impulse build up of its own accord. Just sit there as if mentally saying 'You want to sneeze? Ok, go ahead, but you won't get any help from me.' Sure enough your sneeze will build up and happen, but there will be a distinct moment of separation between your will and the overwhelming will of the sneeze. I don't think it is exaggerating to say that this moment brings with it a sense of 'I'. A sense of something separate and in control, that doesn't have to be carried away immediately by a powerful impulse. This detached sense of 'Me' is a vital psychic tool. I hope this sneezing example isn't too trivial to reveal it. The inner poise required not to get overwhelmed and excited by your early visual hallucinations brings a gentle and pleasant feeling of security.

5 *Having become aware that what you are looking for lies beyond the first, pleasant visual magic, continue to concentrate on your speculum until the cloudiness and pinpoints of light disappear.*

You will then begin to see definite forms. These could be quite dramatic. Faces old and young, coloured landscapes and vistas, objects, flowers and natural images of all kinds. The more calm and quiet and balanced your mind is the more these visions will present themselves.

You are getting close, but note the following. It would be a great mistake to take these visions personally, don't be in a hurry to attribute meaning to any of them too quickly. They arise and fade for many reasons. Like the sneeze exercise above, don't be too eager to leap off your perch and get excited or involved. It is as if you have just opened a window on to a crowded street, but the crowd actually has nothing particularly to do with you. You are experiencing a kind of waking dream. Your speculum has focused on its images from deep inside you. You must now find the images that are meaningful.

6 *As the images pass by, you will find that some are accompanied by a much more definite feeling.*

These are the important ones. This definate feeling is a sense of knowing. These images contain the psychic potential and predictions that you are looking for. If you get only one image straight away, all well and good.

7 *Now that you have some psychic impressions to work with, the next step is to understand and benefit from what you have seen. You must naturally look for sense in what the speculum shows you. If you don't, you will get wildly excited by what you see, and simply rush about telling people you have a secret knowledge or power, or some such fantasy.*

For the speculum as for your dreams, the best way to sort out the genuine psychic impressions that are addressed to you personally, from psychic 'chaff' is to develop sincere specific questions in your mind and see how your impressions answer them.

When you progress to doing readings for clients, you will need to rely very much on your clear knowledge-carrying images. Your clients will have very specific questions wherever possible.

I should explain at this point that certain recurring symbols do arise in crystal ball or speculum readings. Some psychics regularly use this symbol approach. Seeing the objects and situations as symbols is valid. After some experience, you will discover that certain objects are revealed to you prior to, or associated with, certain types of event. For example, a psychic may see blue flowers, whenever someone in their family is going to have a success of some sort. Another person will see a black car tyre, whenever they are about to take an unnecessary or incautious risk. It takes time and some record-keeping to establish the meanings of certain images for you personally, but it can be done, and for many this is a part of their way of interpreting and predicting. Whatever you do, don't rely on anyone else's lists of symbolic meanings, and certainly don't buy a book of symbols for this reason. Objects mean different things to different people. Develop a symbol code of your own.

Some readers see absolutely nothing in their crystal or speculum, but become aware of a distinct emotion or impression. For them the ball is simply an aid to focusing their concentration and is not visual. If you get results you are happy with this way, forget scrying and follow your particular talent.

After you have done some scrying on your own, try it with a sympathetic friend. After a while, it is easy to become too theoretical, working alone, and to get discouraged. Your enthusiasm will rouse you to greater heights with the presence of a friend. You will be surprised, and so will they at the connections and insights your new found powers of crystal ball reading will show. Remember to end with the usual closing down process.

Direct clairvoyance (Being psychic)

How often it happens. The phone rings and you 'just know' immediately who it is going to be. There are many such occasions, when you 'just know', either what has happened or is going to happen:

You pull up at a strange petrol station, and just know that the man taking the cash is going to have a moustache and glasses. Sure enough there he is, complete with handlebars and horn-rims. You look out of the window and one second later a bird lands on the ledge as if to meet your eyes. You just knew it was going to be there.

You lose a book, and later find another copy of it.

You speak, and voice exactly the thought that was occurring to your friend.

We all know what it is like to be psychic in such small ways. Direct clairvoyance is knowing things without referring to any source, such as a crystal. It sounds impossible to cultivate further, but there are techniques as in all the other methods I have described so far. All the above examples happen to professional psychics no more often than they do to ordinary folk. But professional psychics train their sensitivity so that they can see connections in daily events that the average person is not aware of.

So how and where do you develop this direct ability to perceive facts at a psychic level? The answer is with people. Psychic readers train themselves in the art of direct clairvoyance as I use the term here. If you develop it, you will be simply learning how to give another person the benefit of what your sensitivity to them has provided. If you have done some of the earlier exercises in the book, which were designed to give you insight into yourself, rather than other people, you will now find that you already possess a store of understandings about yourself that will apply just as much to other people as it does to you. Your sensitivity to yourself and the forces around you will have put you in an ideal position to try this most direct and sensitive of psychic techniques.

The 'object' you are going to read while doing direct clairvoyance is not a speculum of any kind. A person is going to be the focus of your psychic abilities. You will deliberately tune in, concentrate on, and read their being. As in the other traditional techniques, you will receive a series of psychic impressions that it is then your task to interpret for them.

Ways of interpreting

I will now describe for you the sort of ways of looking, thinking and talking that a responsible and competent psychic would use, if requested to do this type of reading. First, however, a quick word about what I am not going to do, until the next chapter any way. Many well-known psychics attribute what they come to know and say, to 'the spirits of the departed'. They have spirit 'guides' who give them wordly information, often through inner voices audible only to them (clairaudience). This line of psychic 'just knowing' requires careful and respectful handling, and will be dealt with later.

So what is there in a person's being that you can tune into? Well, the first thing you can decide about your potential subject is: are they good or bad. Don't judge them. Just decide, is this person good or bad *for me*? If they have a pleasant effect on you, or no effect at all, well and good. If you feel that they have a bad effect on you, however, seriously consider not doing a reading for them.

You will be aware that inside every person are the forces that made them what they are in their daily lives. Now, this reservoir of human experience stands before you, waiting to reveal itself. In a way, you are going to have to open *yourself* up and let *their* feeling enter into you. Do you want to do this with this person? If you don't, simply decline to read for them. Make an excuse about your inexperience or the phases of the moon. Take all the blame, but *don't read for them.*

In doing direct clairvoyance, more than any other technique, you must be secure in yourself, or another's feelings may shake you. A conscious sense of who you are must be very clear now, like a counterweight. Imagine a plank jutting out over a cliff. The more weight there is on the terra firma end, the further out into the unknown you can venture. Your sense of 'me' is like that counterweight. Hold it to you, secure and safely defined, and you will be able to loosen up and sensitize to your client's deepest nature, to climb out into thin air and pluck the psychic impressions you are looking for.

Incidently, it is this emphatic sense of identity, that makes many a professional psychic seem eccentric or wildly egotistic. Their often large, charismatic egos are mainly there as ballast! Feel free to develop your own idiosyncracies, habits and rituals in your psychic work. This will strengthen your feeling of security in psychic realms.

EXERCISE: Knock-knock

Here is a very short, fun-to-do exercise to remind you yet again of your vital sense of 'me'.

In many situations, it is a polite habit to knock on someone's door before entering. Your knock is simply a request for their consent to enter.

1 *Next time you are in a room, and someone who knows you're*
  there knocks to come in . . . completely ignore them!

This isn't easy. You will probably be taken from a state of relative
calm, to a condition of guilt and a host of other nail-biting
conditions, with every repeated knock! But what this exercise
achieves, is to gather into one place all your feelings, thoughts, and
just about every other mental aspect of you. Within seconds you
will be very much more concentrated in *you*.

2 *With every knock you will become even more aware of yourself*
  until it becomes unbearable. Let them in and make your excuses,
  if they haven't barged in anyway!

Don't do this trick too often or your reputation for general
reliability and even for sanity could suffer.

   Once a professional psychic has agreed to read for a client he/she
will set aside some time and a quiet place that suits the situation.
This is what happens next:

   The place to start a reading is with the voice, which reveals all.
It is possible to follow the stream of a person's voice right back into
their deepest heart, often well beyond where they themselves have
been. Many stage psychics rely on very little more than the voice to
gain impressions. (You have already done listening exercises in
Chapters Three and Six, so you can look back to that and remind
yourself of how to tune in.) The difference here is largely only a
question of degree.

   From the voice you can tell:

If a person is happy or depressed.

If they are pretending to be what they are not.

Whether they are nervous or trying to be strong.

Whether soft or aggressive.

Their whole character is in the sound they make, regardless of what
words they utter.

Are they positive or negative?

Harsh or grating?

Are their attitudes open or closed?

You need have no fear of making unjustified assumptions of quite a
deep and sweeping nature about a person's character, based solely

on voice. The list of what it can reveal is long. In practice it takes a few seconds of listening with your inner sensitivity control turned up to the maximum. You may be left with an impression such as: 'This person sounds afraid' or 'I can hear disappointment,' or, more positively, 'How gently they show themselves.' You can also feel in yourself the emotion that underlies the voice:

Warmth

Anxiety

Pride

Self-doubt

Impatience

People's normal everyday voices, even when they are saying commonplace things like 'A pound of onions please,' are full of such emotions. A person does not have to shout to be expressing anger in their voice. Nor do they have to talk about their lover, in order to express affection. For the beginner, it's all down to knowing what's there, and looking hard.

This last feel-it-yourself impression of voice is the best in my opinion. When this happens, you will find it hard to say anything conscious, you will just mentally note that this person has made you feel something of themselves by their voice. Its meaning will surface later in your reading.

It is a psychic fact, that voices are visible too! If you close your eyes and listen closely to a voice, it is quite possible for a vision of that voice to appear in your mind's eye. All sounds can produce a visual response. Do the following exercise, if you feel the need to prove the principal. Knowing that seeing sound is a fact will encourage you to focus your psychic sensitivities in this area.

EXERCISE: Seeing sound

Sit down in a quiet place, and get comfortable. You are going to visualize a green boat floating gently on a blue sea.

1 *Close your eyes, relax and see vividly in your mind's eye the scene as nearly as you can. If your colours turn out to be different, that is fine.*

2 *Now, get a friend to suddenly make a very loud noise quite close to you! Perhaps two dustbin lids banged together?*

I realize that the anticipation factor will make this a difficult thing to get together, but if you do manage it, your peaceful mental picture will not just disappear upon the loud sound bursting in. A distinct pattern of shapes, or forms, with a colours and patterns of their own will tear into the picture suddenly and then disappear a fraction of a second later, along with the main picture.

3 *Once you know that sounds convert into visible shapes, you can perhaps close your eyes at some later point in a reading, and see if anything springs into your visual mind.*

The sight of a person's voice brings with it certain insights into their nature, and deeper motives. You can see hidden feelings and moods by simply tuning into the colours you perceive.

4 *The shapes, too, are revealing.*

Some people have voices that look like stacks of square frames, gold and vibrating very fast, but highly regular and organized. Others speak in irregular folding green waves, that seem to roll over and become top-heavy! It takes practice, but it is possible, and worth aiming for. And compared to the work required to become say a competent astrologer, or a homeopath it is insignificant! There is so much more to say about the voice but we must move on.

5 *By now you will have an impression. You must express it quickly.*

Avoid inertia, because this causes impressions to build up in your mind, overlap and then dissolve altogether. If you don't give voice to an impression as soon as it arrives it will fade forever and you will be left with a feeling that you've missed a good opportunity. What's more, this feeling of loss will block out the next impression. And the cycle will continue. Inertia is no friend of psychic sensitivity. You musn't lapse into dark silences. Light silences yes. Happy silences, where your psychic perception is active, too active perhaps to permit you to speak easily . . . yes. But not dark inertias, in which you feel yourself falling asleep, or brooding about what you might have said two sentences ago. Some psychics deliberately make reading a very agitated and high energy situation. They talk incessantly, and seem to be almost hyper-active. You don't have to adopt this style, but if you lapse into beginner's doldrums, be prepared to go into psychic overdrive, to get yourself out. If it's any consolation, people expect a psychic to be a bit unconventional. You don't have to justify yourself to your client. If you feel that you're blocked up, or whatever phrase describes your feelings of inertia, wave your hands about, vigorously if necessary, to get back on the wave of positive expression. Fast and vigorous hand gestures and even arm movements will help. Shake off inertia when it arrives, and maintain a steady stream of expression, to keep it at bay.

When you have received a visual feeling from the voice of your client . . . a colour perhaps, proceed as follows:

6 *Look for colours or impressions of colour (the human aura)*
emanating from their body.

We all have an aura. Now compare what you have seen in the voice picture with what you see of the aura and interpret as follows. The voice aura is the past, and the body aura is the future. That is, what has shown itself psychically in their voice is their predisposition, what they are most of the time; what they show in their body aura is their intention, what they want, or want to become.

Remember the earlier exercise where you were asked to find in yourself certain mood-responses to certain colours? You will have to direct this colour feel on to voice and aura, in order to make a true psychic comparison, but more of that stage soon. The above is one personal technique and it can be adapted to suit your own psychic perceptions and talents. Before I explain this final stage, a word about the aura.

The aura

The author and many psychics have seen the aura, so whether it exists isn't open to debate. What is open to debate is what it means. In my opinion there is only one way of interpreting the colours and forms that radiate in and out of all human bodies and voices. It is from personal experience. Just like all the other psychic realities we have dealt with, the interpretations must be evolved by the individual who sees them. The cycle goes: first sensitize yourself, next perceive psychically and, lastly, interpret in the light of your own experience. It is an enclosed and private process in which you are never going to be any more than a learner.

If, for example, you have only seen one aura in your life, in the form of a pink, sparkling glow around the head of an enthusiastic friend who is speaking about a new neighbour . . . you can draw your own conclusions. Pink auras around the head equal affection, hope, enthusiasm, talking about new developments, anticipation. The more you learn about the person with the aura, the more you will develop your understanding of what they were feeling at the moment you saw the psychic light coming from them. Perhaps it turns out that they are looking forward to talking to this new person largely because they themselves are feeling slightly mentally frustrated. The newcomer is perhaps a minister with a reputation for being inspiring. Immediately you sense the possibility of a kind of religious significance in the pinkness. I'm sure you see the process.

Or take the following example. You are visiting a friend in hospital. The doctor or specialist walks into the room. As he reaches to pull the curtain around the bed, a green light seems to hover near his waist. On the way out one of the nurses smiles at you and you see a light pink and green haze near her head. What could you but think? Green and healers go together. And then a strange thing happens. One day, the lady who runs the corner shop also shows green near her as you say good morning. She is no doctor! Then, later, you see her feeding a stray cat with great concern and sympathy. You conclude that green perhaps means broader things than just doctors and nurses and healing.

The human aura is not fixed. It fluctuates and shifts as different thoughts and emotions pass through the mind. Colours and shapes that come about like this are called thought-forms. Everyone produces thought-forms. They tend to be fleetingly visible around the head, especially at moments of emotional intensity. Once again let me direct you back to earlier exercises, when I was telling you how to see the forms associated with natural processes of growth and decay. Do the same intense focusing on people and expect visual forms to become apparent. A good situation to start observing for thought forms is in any place where people are in a mood of anticipation.

Auras, like policemen, are easy to find when you are not looking for them! A direct attempt to get one inevitably sends them in the opposite direction. I'm sure you know about such phenomena. Taxis, and parking places embody a similar psychic truth, always abounding when unwanted. Many things in the world of desire are like this. They arrive just when you've not so much given up wanting them, but completely forgotten about them altogether! To see the elusive aura, try a combination of entering your trance state, and using the well tried glancing technique. Instead of looking at the person, look straight past them, and casually glance toward them and away.

It's not so much the movement of your eyes that constitutes a casual glance, it is your state of mind. You somehow deliberately put a lot of your concentration in the opposite direction from your subject, but keep a kind of peripheral focus on anything that might vaguely be occurring near their end of your awareness. Soft, even lighting helps.

Between this and whatever relaxtion/trance technique you favour you are bound to be able to trick your rational brain into letting a fleeting impression of an aura or a thought-form through. And fleeting it will be. Don't expect people to light up and stay that way, or for large halos to fix themselves over your subject. Be quick in your perceptions and dwell carefully and long on the slightest hint of an impression. Just because famous psychics and visionaries write books about — or paint dramatic pictures of — their visions, does not mean that their wonderful gifts were solid, permanent hallucinations; more likely the complete opposite. Their vision was so fleeting and tantalizing, that the psychic felt compelled to somehow capture it and give it a greater semblance of permanence, the better to learn from it. I explain this to help you validate your own fragile first experiences which, as early psychic impressions, are easily brushed off as coincidences or tricks of the light. Look for auras in the ways suggested and you will see them.

So far in your reading you have heard the voice, seen the voice, seen the aura, compared the voice (past) with the aura (future), and looked for thought forms as they arise (present). Now continue your technique as follows.

A symbol

Request your inner psychic vision to give you some sort of symbol. It could be anything but, whatever you see, interpret it symbolically. Don't tell your sitter what you have seen. Use your vision as a basis for discussing any problems, predictions or statements that have arisen out of the previous observations. Talk around it as it were, and try to apply any of the qualities of the symbol vision to whatever your sitter says. For example:

Your client's voice was elated, perhaps too elated. It made you feel brittle and defensive. (You are not being brittle and defensive, these are the feelings you are picking up! You are secure, poised and psychically sensitized.)

The voice had a grey appearance and its shape was spiky.

The body aura showed a plain yellowness around the head.

You somehow felt that the voice was much more complex than the body. There was something missing. Grey you know is a protective colour.

At the mention of children, a blackness enters the voice and the head glows reddish.

You feel anger rise up in you, but suddenly the yellow grows strong again. You suspect a dispute involving a child and you are right. The return of the yellow suggests that good sense and reason will prevail, but the loss feeling is still there.

Now you call in the last part of the technique. You request a symbol. It comes in the form of a loaf of bread on a plate! The client talks about what he is going to do in a custody dispute. You suggest he concentrate on being the provider (bread).

The discussion continues about a woman. You mention perfume or a smell (bread). The client seems happier, more resolved.

You suggest he is looking for something to do with the earth (bread) . . . a home? He seems excited. His body aura fills out, and becomes a kind of orange-green.

The effect of your symbol and its interpretation seems to be bringing texture to the aura, and to the voice, bringing them into more of a balance. Because your symbol seemed to produce a good effect in the auras, you feel confident to suggest to him that he will succeed.

Only when you have received your symbol, and tried it out in this way — by looking back again at the body aura and the voice, and the relationship between all three — can you speak an outcome. You judge the probable outcome from the psychic signs: past (voice) present tendencies (aura), and future or possible future (your symbol vision). If the first two are rendered more in harmony by the third, you are at liberty to give a good prediction. If they are unclear, say nothing.

The above is only a very general guide, but it is a framework and a technique within which you can work. It is, I know, very visual. But, for example, with the above person you might suddenly get the strong impression of a name or a number. As a psychic reader you will have to take risks, so blurt this out as it arrives. Don't use it as a symbol, or try to elaborate on it.

When you meet new people, try out your non-visual powers right away. See if any particular impressions strike you. A place name, a type of landscape, a house or an animal — anything. With a bit of careful fishing, you can often get an idea of how close you were, and slowly build up and notice any recurring symbols that come to have meaning.

Another good exercise is to try to tell your friends about their parents or grandparents. They will soon confirm if you are right in any way. They will also wonder why you are asking, so you expect to have to come out of the closet a bit about your psychic hopes and fears. The thing about many non-visual psychic readers is that they tend to allude so much to 'voices' and spirit guides speaking inwardly. The readings seem to be characterized by being extremely rambling and often full of seemingly trivial information. (No disrespect intended.) My spirit guide is not the slightest bit interested in whispering to me insights about the hidden side of other people's lives, so I am at a loss to recommend a technique from experience. However, more about spirits, and what they can and can't do for your psychic powers here on earth, follows in the next chapter.

Experiment with the basic people reading technique outlined above. Its vagueness is deliberate, as it will encourage you to start direct clairvoyance, and won't ham-string you with too many do's and don'ts. In the end your own natural sensitivity will shine through in your own way.

At the end of your session, be sure to close down your psychic sensitivity. Do all the usual earthly things you have done after previous exercises, only more so. Some practical gesture such as returning the chairs in the room to their original place, or gently re-arranging the lighting will always be best. You can't close down too clearly or too firmly, so feel free to invent your own 'grounding' and winding up procedures. One last point: as always, do leave your client with good news whatever it takes to do so!

10
THE WORLD
OF SPIRITS

This chapter is probably going to be rather controversial. Let me say from the start that it is not my intention to offend anybody's religious convictions. I realize that there are those who regard this aspect of psychic awareness as completely taboo. They have their beliefs and consider psychic practices that deal with the sensitive matter of death and any possible existence beyond it to be presumptious. And there will be others who think it merely preposterous.

However, there are also many people who, having had some psychic experience, are sincerely inclined to accept the possibility of something other than a sudden blank wall at the moment of death of their physical body. Such psychically attuned people have developed a confident feeling for a reality that takes place slightly beyond what is only to do with the body and the impressions of their physical senses. The idea of continuing their experience over into a dimension where they are able to deal with spirits, 'intelligences' which do not have bodies, is not a very great leap for them. If you have been regularly experiencing the inexplicable, and technically impossible, in the form of quiet knowledge that comes to you from no logical place, you soon feel free to extend your enquiries into anywhere that you feel might be fruitful. Worrying that you are crossing some impossible limitation (in this case death) does not really come into it: you've already crossed the boundaries of what is possible or impossible many times before.

Your inner psychic experience conditions you away from your body, and into a dimension where you feel the movement of your thoughts and higher emotions more strongly. This body-free inner life is a very real domain for the psychic. Clairvoyant awareness can take place in a pitch dark room, with ears blocked, and nothing happening at all. In fact, such environments have been deliberately arranged, in the form of 'sensory deprivation tanks'. These are tanks of water, maintained at body temperature, and with all light and sound excluded. The occupant lies suspended in fluid at body temperature, positioned so that they can feel no sensation at all; no touch, no pressure, weight or even the heat of their own body.

The overwhelming impression reported by people, clairvoyant or not, who have spent even a few minutes disconnected from the world in this way is interesting. They do not report any feelings of a lessening of their experience, as you might expect. Quite the reverse, they are often overwhelmed by the increasing intensity of what happens to them. Taking the senses away, opens the door to a completely new and often beautiful world of inner realities. By all accounts though, it doesn't do to stay in such deprivation tanks for long. The pull for the natural world of daylight, sound and touch is irresistible. Human awareness naturally cries out to be firmly in its body, with all its senses operating. However, anyone who has had such an experience will know that there can quite easily be very intense awareness existing without the necessity of body. What's more, the less body there is, the more intense seems to be the awareness.

It is precisely such bodiless forms of awareness that I am going to deal with when talking about spirits. There are existing organized bundles of awareness which do not have physical bodies. They are awareness without body, and I refer to them as spirits.

Human spirits

In the chapter on the body you will remember how I described the head in derogatory terms. This was done deliberately, to help any potential psychic person to get away from the idea of their head being the centre of their being. In passing, I'd like to say that an old Red Indian term of ridicule for a person regarded as insane was: 'He thinks with his head!' It is a very recent and superficial conception to imagine that your human intelligence is located in your head. Therefore, in order to direct your perceptions to richer psychic areas, I drew attention to the psychic realities present in other parts of the body.

In this chapter, I am going to direct you to the possibility that awareness has an even broader focus. Your awareness, even your actual intelligence and specific knowledge, does not originate in your head. Neither is it from your body. It comes to you from a dimension of spirit. It is the sensation of this spiritual dimension entering into you and living in you, that you experience as awareness. Consider the following example.

A compass needle shows evidence of intelligence of a kind. It behaves in a logical way and always points to the north. If you showed this phenomenon to a very simple-minded person, they might quite understandably conclude that there was something in the needle that made it behave in this remarkable way. But anyone who knows anything about the magnetic field surrounding the earth, will understand immediately that a greater force, one that is present all around, acts, and shows itself in the seemingly intelligent behaviour of the needle.

This is very much what happens with our awareness. We narrow our awareness too much, thinking it is in one place at one time and in one thing. Actually, it is present and active in much broader realms than we are in the habit of looking into.

It isn't a good idea generally to look to science for support for personal psychic experience, but here is an exception. There are carefully controlled experiments on animal learning patterns that are beginning to 'prove' the existence of intelligence outside the body:

In laboratory tests on rats it has been discovered that a rat will do a simple task considerably quicker if other rats before it have repeated and mastered the same task.

Once one rat has solved a problem, other rats that follow, having been kept completely separate, somehow know what the first rat has learned. They approach the task with a distinct advantage, and solve it quicker.

The supernaturally acquired knowledge also enters into awareness of totally unrelated rats, that were unborn at the time of the experiment!

The scientific name chosen for this universal reservoir of rat intelligence is 'the morpho-genetic field'. A more superstitious label would perhaps be 'the great rat spirit in the sky'. What, after all, is in a name?

One last reference to the scientific world before moving on to much closer matters. If you look at any solid object under an electron microscope (the strongest microscope in existence), you find that it is made up of varying electric charges and particles in constant movement. Anything, whether it be a rock, a glass, even our skin and bone, though solid to the senses, turns out to be a surging sea of electric charges. These charges and particles, although in constant movement, manage to avoid colliding with each other in total chaos, and combine and move in very stable and organized ways. It is the fact that they organize themselves in such a careful way that gives the impression of solidity. One cannot look at such a potential for complete chaos as it slots perfectly together, without the thought arising that there must be *something* that knows exactly where each little particle should go and when. An intelligence organizes the entire performance. Modern science has not the remotest idea how to approach this intelligence. It is unable to frame any suitable question to elicit a single clue as to what it is that keeps all this potential whirling chaos in such perfect harmony. But the answer, of course, is 'spirit'. Spirit controls matter and not the other way round. If you want to approach spirit and understand it, you must acknowledge its superiority and do a quick mental turn about. Then you have to wait enquiringly and see how much of itself it wants to make plain to you. Spirit is understanding; and it understands you and your understandings better than you do!

One last example. You are with the above simple-minded person from the previous compass example! He sees some tyre marks in the dust and asks, what is it? You say a car was here. Oh, he says, which way was it going? You are able to tell him. He is impressed. He asks if it was going fast, and was it a big car . . . again you enlighten him with some certainty!

Then he asks you what colour it was! You are unable to say. He then asks you who was in it? You tell him you have no idea. He begins to lose his faith in you as a reliable source of information!

Being a simple person he might even feel slightly resentful of you for seeming so magically all-knowing at first, and then letting him down. The rational mind is very much like this disappointed person.

The truth of the matter is that it is not you, the answer-supplying person, but he himself who is falling short. There comes a point in his questioning where his questions become the very things that cause him to feel the lack of satisfactory answers! He is unaware of it, but his questions start merely to demonstrate his ignorance in the whole business. They emphasize nothing more than his own lack of real understanding of what is actually going on in the situation. Even worse, his dismissive attitude to the answer now blocks him from being so open to any further explanations being directed his way. He feels so sure that he has made enquiries to the limits of what is available to be known.

These examples are simply to help you grasp two basic ideas.

The force of spirit in the world is real and actual; moral forces are as powerful in every way as physical ones.

Do not be short changed by 'authorities' of one kind or another who insist that spirits are unknowable. Spirits, both with and without bodies, are knowable.

The appreciation of spirits is all but lost to the modern age, but the idea of spirit has been with humanity for as far back as human history can be traced, in every culture and in every part of the world.

In former times men concentrated on evolving an understanding of the influence of spiritual beings just as today the effects of material knowledge draw people's minds.

I am sure that everyone can attach some meaning to the word 'angel'. It is a spirit. To popular thinking one that has wings, and a halo around its head, and generally is shining and good. Such is the popular idea of an angel. In short, there is still some current understanding of the possibility of a spiritual being, called an angel. The language at least provides a label for such an entity.

In earlier times, for many generations, people all over the planet studied in a very sincere and far from ignorant way the possibilities of angels and all they stood for; they learned much. They became aware of other spirits; in fact, an entire hierarchy was discovered. The Christian Church, which came to be the authority in this part of the world — and as such the equivalent of the Department of Science — evolved labels for the different spiritual beings that came to be perceived. Angels were the least of them. Above angels were Archangels, and above them were beings they called Principalities.

It didn't stop there. Continued spiritual research brought to light another strata of beings, called Powers, Mights, and Dominions. And above them, even mightier intelligences, given the names of Thrones, Cherubim, and Seraphim. Other cultures came to similar conclusions (with slight variations) and evolved their own terms of reference. These labels were not evolved out of sheer fantasy. Not all people were researching upwards towards beings that were above humanity. Spirits of chaos were found with ugly names and intentions. They, too, had hierarchies which seemed to mirror the upwards strata of the divine beings. Lucifer, the fallen angel; a spirit called Ahriman, who operated below Lucifer; Beelzebub, or Mephistopheles — a combination of the two. And the lowest of the low, which were mentioned more in Eastern spiritual studies, dark beings called the Asuras.

A range of beings on the borders between humanity and the upward and downward hierarchies were also noticed. These were — and still are — called Elementals. They are the forces of the elements of fire, air, earth, and water. An elemental is a spirit that shows itself in the physical world, in the activity of one of the elements. The names of the elemental spirits are: Gnomes, Undines, Sylphs, and Salamanders (earth, water, air and fire). In among these were woven the regional variations of folklore and the observations of rural researchers: the Fairies and Pixies, the Elves and Goblins, the manikins and mermaids, and many more are to be found here.

There were also added to this organized perception of spirits, the Ghosts, Wraiths, Spectres and Phantoms, each with their own particular qualities.

Are we to assume that all this body of knowledge is today totally meaningless? I don't think so. Oddly though, the spiritual research that goes under that name today, seems to ignore most of what is available to clairvoyant sight. Modern psychic research focuses around but one tiny spirit possibility. Psychics seem to have become stuck on attempting to contact the individual human spirit after death. Angels or fire spirits are of no interest, but the ghost of Aunt Ethel who passed on 50 years ago is! There is a kind of poverty in this. With all the many different spirit forces to investigate, it is surprising that we are so interested in encountering the spirit of one single human and strain to detect its commonplace, and often confused reports. Surely, our lifetimes provide the best opportunity for communicating with the spirits of our fellow men and women.

Spiritualism

If you get the chance, visit a Spiritualist Church. Such churches exist all over the world, and are a great source of inspiration for psychic awareness. But you must tread very cautiously to get the best for your own development in them. The people involved in them are extremely friendly and should be treated with the respect and deference due to sincere, spiritually aspiring people.

However, at the basis of spiritualist activity, is not so much a delusion, as a lack of accurate focus. They see the barrier between life on earth and life not-on-earth, as very relevant. Death is their focus, and is seen by them as something to be triumphed over. Their ultimate good is to give proof of the fact that death is just a doorway to a new world. They are frequently very successful in coming up with this proof too! If you want to see some of this evidence, go to a spiritualist church for yourself, and find out. I recommend it as highly beneficial to the growth of your psychic awareness. Whatever you do though, go in a mood of respect and humility, not as an arrogant researcher demanding to know the facts of their beliefs and so on. There are many psychically gifted and compassionate mediums you can listen to and learn from. (You will also encounter a number of well meaning bluffers.)

Spiritualist services are open to the public, and usually last about an hour-and-a-half. They usually begin with a devotional, but not necessarily 'Christian' opening, including hymns, prayers, and readings from the scriptures. They end with an address and individual clairvoyant readings and messages, delivered by either one of the resident sensitives, or a visiting one. Even a total newcomer may get a message from the spirit world and the atmosphere is definitely one to be experienced.

The techniques most often used are psychometry, spirit vision, and clairaudience or spirit voices. Prayer to the spirit is the way of progress most Spiritualists recommend. Try the following techniques for yourself.

Clairaudience

The best practical starting point from which a mentally healthy person can cultivate clairaudience is to use the sea-shell method detailed on page 144. It will be best if you have also tried and understand some of the other techniques at some length. As in the direct clairvoyance, and the crystal ball reading, you will find that

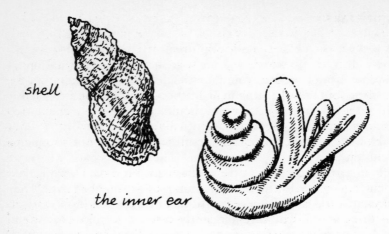

shell

the inner ear

a combination of relaxation and deliberate creation of atmosphere will bring results. The atmosphere you want to surround yourself with is one of stillness and purity of intention. I can't offer any other suggestions on specific ways of achieving 'atmosphere' without confusing as many readers as I might help. Experienced psychics prepare with reverence. They don't just sit down and expect their spirit voices to come through. So don't you expect to! If voices occur at any other time than when you have sat and prepared yourself, and are consciously trying to hear them, I recommend you go to see your doctor. Psychic knowledge is not for you yet.

1 *Seat yourself in a quiet place, close your eyes and attempt to enter as deep and still a state of mind as you can.*

2 *Now put your concentration to the right, lower side of your head, to a point outside you, in the region of your right ear.*

3 *Now simply wait.*

Many report that their voices seem to come as if from one consistent physical direction. When on stage, the late Doris Stokes would always listen to her right for voices, and always her husband would sit in that quarter as if to provide inspiration and love. Listening on the right is at least a starting point for concentration but when the voices come, they may not actually come from there, so don't block anything out from elsewhere.

Spirit voices may be vague and indistinct, surprising or hard to understand, but they should always be heartwarming, and inspiring. If unpleasant auditory hallucinations are induced, ignore them. They often take the form of harshly spoken statements and groups of words. These are not to be dwelt on. They arise as a result of the mechanism of the brain doing what it does in a dream. It takes a perfectly ordinary sound, like the scraping of a car door outside, and converts it into something entirely different. The visual fantasy works on such a sound, and creates from it, say, a dream image of a lion roaring.

In the partial dream state into which you have put yourself, your mind can create speech out of such noises. It is very easy to forget when you wake that there even was an original sound. You might just remember some harsh syllables spoken in a very dead voice, and not the metallic rasp that they were originally. The often cold and lifeless tones of such speech hallucinations are due to the fact that warmth and human expression are entirely absent from the original noise. In your sensitized state this is highly obvious, and the speech that arises reflects this non-human quality.

Try hard to find in your memory a trace of the physical sound that started your hallucination. When a voice comes, it will be gentle, and probably a complete surprise to you. And quite rightly. Hearing voices in your head is a sign of incipient madness, and it is to be hoped that you are perfectly sane! Try to be content with one or two very clear and undeniable statements. There are no doubts about the reality of such statements in so far as they are just like real voices, in real language, only no actual person is present to say them.

As to what you do as a result of any information they contain, or how you interpret them, I make one clear suggestion. Wait patiently and see what unfolds. You have made yourself open and have heard something. You need feel no urge or responsibility to do anything else. Unless you want to go a long way down the road of professional mediumship, I do not recommend that you cultivate any relationship with these voices, or what they say. Spiritualist mediums refer to them as their guides, and speak very warmly about them and the things they reveal. If you want to do this I strongly recommend that you seek the advice of a developed Spiritualist medium.

The above technique is to help you develop confidence in discovering your unknown abilities, not to encourage you to conduct dialogues with voices in your head. The gentle listening in to the sounds of the shell, I recommend as much more inspiring to psychic growth. There is a whole world of sound lying just under the surface of its gentle murmur, and often a message of great purity comes straight through to the heart from it. I have received many more meaningful messages in the psychic content of the sounds of nature than in any of the cryptic statements from spirit voices. Go out into the countryside, sit down and deliberately tune into the sound of water, or bird song, and your psychic ears will become vastly more sensitive than by listening to the spirit voices. That is my opinion anyway.

What is death?

Spiritualism is inextricably associated with death, so let's try to dwell happily on this subject for a while. What happens when we die? Over the last hundred years The Society for Psychical Research has amassed a large and respectable body of evidence on this question. Suspending disbelief for a moment, many spirit accounts from people who have died, and who report back via respected mediums, are consistent and very specific on the whole business of life after death.

According to those who have experienced it, death by natural causes happens over a period of days. It is a peaceful affair, though it may appear distressing to onlookers. The deceased say that they spend their last hours gently withdrawing into consciousness, often seeing visions of friendly 'golden figures', or family, lovers and friends who have died before them. Eventually they 'wake up', surrounded and greeted by welcoming loved ones and others un-recognized yet somehow familiar.

Most accounts are very clear on one point though. Apparently, we reach the other side in the same state of mind as we left this one. Some posthumous witnesses express disappointment about this. Death doesn't seem to have been the absolute thing they were hoping for. Simply an altered state of consciousness. Memory banks are intact, and personality habits that they might have preferred to shake off are all still firmly with them!

They find themselves in a dimension where matter is of so fine a texture that they can mould it merely by thinking. From their earthly memories, newly dead people, according to theory, choose for themselves a shape matching the one they had when they were happiest in this life. From then on they create around them whatever they can conceive in their imaginations to enjoy, until eventually they desire to advance and learn new understandings.

The moment of death is accompanied by a tableau of memory images that plays their whole life backwards for them.

There are, of course, many other perceptions of the events of death. The main point to make though is that to a psychically inclined person the veil between life and death is quite thin. If you want to experience by experiment how thin it is you can do so.

The first thing to do is to look at the actual word death. It always brings with it very physical feelings of decay, darkness and loss. It is without a doubt the wrong word for the condition of consciousness that arises when your physical body stops functioning. Actually, to psychic perception the dead are no more dead than the living. One of the psychic techniques mentioned earlier involves mentally shutting out all perception of the physical body in order to see a deeper reality. What you can receive from a living person, when you achieve this, you could just as well receive from a so-called 'dead' one. It is the word 'dead' that makes it all sound so distasteful. You can't say it without somehow thinking of a corpse. A 'dead' person, the word insists, is one who is lying cold and still. Not so! That is only a dead body.

Departure of the spirit

Perhaps I could present death in a slightly less morbid way. There is something in us that is more than our physical body. This is beyond argument. At the moment of death, the body starts to break down into the mineral elements out of which it was composed. Obviously, something that was there before — that was preventing this process from occurring — has now withdrawn. Another way of looking at it is that the spirit has departed. This departure of the thing that made the body alive is much regretted, and the body, so familiar and the focus of that person's spirit for so long, begins to act like vegetable matter and decay. The tradition of burying people in the cold black earth does little to alleviate the feeling of oppression and irretrievable loss that surrounds this break-up of the body.

But the loss of the physical is only a result of the spirit separating out from it. A vital living element becomes very apparent in the process. This is the nuance of the whole matter that the word death simply does not convey at all. Death is only half the story. Life is the other half.

In very practical terms then, is it true to say that the spirit, having abandoned the body, is no longer available to be experienced by we body-occupying souls. Does it, too, disappear?

No, it doesn't. Have you ever experienced feelings such as the following?

A person who has recently died comes up in conversation. As you recall them, they may not have been very pleasant. In fact, they may have behaved appallingly toward you. Nevertheless, you find it very hard to bring yourself to speak negatively of them now that they are dead. The reason for this, if you search within yourself, will be found in a deep, unconscious feeling that they are not so far away as you might imagine. You sense that any expression of animosity which you put out into the world, will somehow reach them. It is as if they were there, and could hear you! You can sense this, just as you can sense when someone you know is in the house, but you can't see them. It is as if they are more present, now than when they were alive. They feel closer in a spiritual way.

With people you love and have been close to it is harder to feel this reality. Your focus on their body and its good and bad impressions on you blind you. But as your memories fade, the feel of their spirit becomes stronger. With those who know you knew well and feel a bond with there is traditionally a very special connection between the worlds of the living and the dead.

We go around, assuming that the 'dead' (actually the not-dead-at-all!) are in a superior condition to us here on earth and have a responsibility in some way to get in touch with us and enlighten us.

In fact, the situation is the other way round. The dead (who are really quite alive in their way!) are in fact very keen to hear from us. The impetus to get in touch lies completely in our hands. If there is to be any flow between this dimension and the one of the spirit, it must flow from us to them. The spirits are entitled to messages from us, not vice versa. Furthermore, what proceeds from us to the place of the spirit must be of a positive nature; otherwise it simply passes unperceived.

In other words, good thoughts, feelings and impulses directed toward the spirit world of the 'dead', render our psychic awareness a great deal richer. Just as we are blind to the perception of a huge portion of the higher spirit world in our physical world, so spirits have no means of relating to our personalized, material, ego-centred thoughts (with a few exceptions). But any thought or impulse that is of a high, pure and love-based kind can make itself felt in the world of the spirit, and is received there with great pleasure. In turn the pleasure of the spirit is (sometimes) returned to us in subtle expressions of spiritual awareness and blessing.

This is all psychic fact, and can be experimented with in whatever way you can adapt it to fit in with your personal life. One word though. Please don't use the above as a means of prolonging a connection with a loved one who is deceased, beyond what is healthy and happy. The living are the best company for the living. Death and all thoughts about it should occupy but a tiny part of our psychic life, and only then in order to enhance our understanding and enjoyment of the beautiful world we are living in.

Ghosts

This brings us to the question of ghosts. I am often asked whether I believe in ghosts. I have to answer that I do. However, the trouble arises when you stop to consider exactly what it is we have seen. As your psychic powers grow you will hopefully be able to keep them fully under your control. But there will be times when you become distinctly aware of what people call an 'atmosphere'. Usually, by this they mean a bad atmosphere, and immediately the suggestion arises of hauntings and ghosts.

Traditionally, ghosts are supposed to be the earthbound spirits of the dead. They are usually associated with bloody deeds, graveyards, old houses and the depths of night. They are reputedly menacing figures, endlessly repeating terrible moments in their past lives, or lost souls, too obsessed with earthly pleasures to progress to higher planes. Such is the popular idea of ghosts. To tell the truth, people who ask me if I believe in these fearsome stereotypes seem to be more interested in airing the taboo subject of death than learning about ghosts.

Statistics about such atmospheres and apparitions give a much more mundane perspective on most ghost sightings. Most ghosts seem to have little to do with spirits of the dead. The title of one of The Society for Psychical Research's first studies on apparitions — *Spontaneous Hallucinations of the Sane* — shows a more down-to-earth explanation for the origin of many ghosts. For example, researchers at Duke University, Carolina analyzed 825 well-attested reports of ghostly apparitions. Of these, they discovered, just 80 involved the appearance of a person who was actually dead. But only a tiny few out of the remaining 'spirits' behaved in any way differently from the apparitions of live persons. So it seems that statistically speaking your average ghost is not really strong on purpose or intent towards us, and probably isn't even dead!

There are however, some understandings about ghosts that can help your psychic perceptions, and go some way to removing the thrill of fear that surrounds spirit sightings and atmospheres. Once more referring to the statistics of the above analysis, it seems that ghosts who you recognize usually have a message for you, and probably originate from your own unconscious telepathic powers. Ghosts who you don't recognize will usually be totally disinterested in you and, although they may cause you a chill sensation, will rarely be hostile.

Types of ghosts

There are records of three main types of ghost, each with a particular reason for being there.

Wraiths are individual spirits associated with one particular place for often introverted and personal reasons.

Spectres are apparitions that arise as a result of situations where one individual will has massively overwhelmed another, as in the case of violence or premature death.

The Phantoms come from a more collective act of will overwhelming will. Mass suffering, and group negative feeling lie at the heart of such spirit manifestations.

Ghosts mainly depend on the elementals of the earth spirits to make themselves known. Though water and air spirits are sometimes involved, mainly it is earth. You will find your awareness of atmospheres at its most susceptible in earth situations: cellars, dungeons, old stone houses, wherever physical matter is dense and prevalent. Stone circles and the ground around them is a typical strong earth-spirit place. The theory behind why the earth spirits affect us in this psychic atmospheric way is interesting.

While we are alive we are creatures of spirit in a physical body. As such we are closely connected to the elemental spirits, those intelligences who we see at work in air, fire, earth and water. Our bodies are to some extent theirs. What separates us from them is a sense of 'I'. Our sense of 'I' actually resides in the denser mineral parts of our bodies. If we let our sense of 'I' grow weak, there are certain elemental beings who will be only too happy to slip in and reclaim these parts of our being. The most mineral parts of the body are the bones, and the nervous sytem, including of course the brain. When the 'I' weakens its grasp, for whatever reason, we begin to 'feel things in our bones' as the expression goes. It also gives rise to a sense that we are aware of a different being in our brain.

Normally, the elemental earth spirits have their pleasure in tending to nature and particularly the vegetable kingdom but, as you can see, there are some who are not adverse to slipping into the human kingdom if the chance arises. With the dutiful elementals of earth there comes a definite mood of watching from outside, as if they saw with detached interest all the foibles and ways of people. They look on the affairs of mankind with a certain detached reflection, and keep their distance. But where there is an opportunity created by a weakened or flagging sense of 'I', some of the more spontaneous spirit impulses are irresistibly drawn back into the material that is so familiar to them, the human dense matter. They attempt to participate in human awareness. Usually the results are mild, and obvious, and can be shaken off within seconds by anyone with a strong identity.

Less forceful mental types may experience confusion, so use your openness to atmospheres carefully. Don't dwell on any brooding atmospheres and shake off anything negative as soon as it becomes apparent. Retain only a detached memory of it, pinned firmly on to your sense of who you are, your 'I'. If necessary, 'vote with your feet'. Accept the fact that you are in an unnecessary situation, and do what you would do in any normal situation that was causing you no pleasure . . . get up and go. Your visual imagination can come to your aid here, by helping you to focus your own will and identity by focusing on some powerful image that you love. The benevolent gold pentagram is a good symbol in this respect.

Uplifting experiences

It is a pity that most psychic atmospheres are popularly thought to be to do with the lower energies. Death and hauntings are the least of what can be perceived with a psychic sensitivity. There are the experiences brought on by the higher beings to be looked into and these are as thrilling and uplifting in a vital and playful sense as the others are potentially depressing and morbid. Actually it takes no more psychic effort to open up to these soaring and pure experiences, and it always surprises me why so many psychics seem to focus on the least interesting perceptions open to psychic sight.

It is to the spirits of air and fire that we can first look to see these higher spirits, and know their refreshing atmospheres. The Sylphs and the Salamanders are the traditional names of the higher elementals. Fire and air are the upper elements. We naturally have to turn our psychic inner perceptions upwards to be able to perceive them.

Spirit life is in some ways exactly like our existence here on earth.

As we go through our day certain things catch our attention and give us more or less pleasure. It's a bit like walking down the street on a Saturday, and stopping every now and then to look into the shopwindows that arouse our interest.

Spirit life has this experience in common with us. They, too, move about their particular environment, and find their fulfilment in certain things that present themselves to their spirit awareness. They are attracted to certain spirit qualities, just as we are attracted to material things. The highest spirits are to be found, crowding around enthusiastically and enjoying the celebration of their favourite thing in life.

When I start using terms like 'crowding round' and 'enjoying' in connection with spirits, it will no doubt arouse in you a need to form a mental picture of what these beings actually look like. This you can do. Spirits are not theoretical at all, and it is only theories that you can't form a picture of. Anything that is not a theory can be pictured. But you have to approach the spirits properly to receive this picture.

Higher spirits give no thought to matter, it is of no interest to them; they have grown out of it. I'm sure you know the feeling of this natural disinterest: there is nothing exclusively spirit-world-only about it.

There was probably a time when the sight of a swing or climbing frame would make your heart leap, and prove an irresistible attraction to your young senses. But now, you probably wouldn't even register a playground if one was right in front of you. This is the feeling of effortless, sublime disinterest that the spirit world feels for much of what we concern ourselves with. It simply doesn't register. Spirits of the higher kind occupy themselves with such things as love, wisdom, enjoyment, fulfilment, and harmony. These are the experiences that fill their landscape.

Another thought may help you get some idea of what it is you are trying to perceive in seeing the higher spirits. We humans are essentially receiving creatures. We receive our bodies, our food, our experience, and just about everything else. Nearly all that we call human is a gift in some form. Our receiving nature is built in to us at a deep level.

The higher spirits are quite different in nature. They are totally giving beings. For them, to receive is out of the question. To try to give anything to such a being is ignorance. So if you want to know their nature, you have to make yourself receptive — which is your natural condition — and align yourself about them, or giving out thoughts of enquiry in their direction will simply backfire on you, and produce no proper result. Don't get me wrong; the spirits, particularly the angels, are very keen to associate with mankind. But the way they like to relate to us is not so much through thoughts and feelings; they have plenty of that in their own environment. What they delight in feeling from humans is action and movement. The doing of physical actions with a high directed feeling is one of the best ways of attracting spirits. It is for this reason, that I am now going to recommend two particular earthly environments where you will be most likely to see spirits.

In places of worship and pure ritual.

In gardens.

Both these places are rich in spirits, and psychic ability will flourish here because actions that take place in them are usually done for higher goals than simply to satisfy the ego of the people doing them.

So, if you have read so far, you will find yourself in a garden or ritual place (of which more soon). You are aware that you want to perceive a being that is not interested in your body or anything physical, and is inherently arranged so that it is always giving outwards.

At this point let me suggest you select a garden, rather than a place of ritual. Find some such natural but happily cultivated spot. The more beautiful in the traditional sense the better. Places of pure ritual are few and far between. Sadly most churches, though once strong, are now usually so surrounded by other influences, that the spirits are vague there.

Look around you in the following way. Regard everything you see in your garden as a form of writing, as a description of something, exactly like words on a page. Let me clarify.

This word before you now, this word 'flower', is actually not a flower at all. It is a series of marks on a paper in a shape that makes you have a picture, or at least an idea of a flower in your mind. Nobody is stupid enough ever to think that black marks on a page can be a flower. Having seen the black squiggles, we can — if we want — go out and see, pick and smell a real flower. And all this is fair enough, as far as it goes. To the psychic's perception, however, it doesn't go far enough. No matter how much we look at, hold or smell the real flower we do not feel that what we have before us is the real flower. We get the distinct feeling that there is still something else to it, that is absent. Something compared to which the flower we hold in our hand is as incomplete as the original black and white word 'flower' was, even though we are smelling, holding and looking at our flower. To psychic sight, real flowers are still no more than a form of writing, a code telling us of something else. It's not sad in any way, we just know there is something more.

The reality we are going to slowly learn to read about in all the objects and occurrences that surround us in our material world, in fact in every part of the material world, is the world of spirits. All the experiences we perceive in this garden we find ourselves in are all letters, words and sentences that when understood tell of a world of spirits.

So we sit in our garden and look at everything, 'reading' the activities of spirits. By reading the garden like this we will gain knowledge of spirit thoughts and, intentions and, ultimately, they will reveal their very appearance.

The best spirits to start off with are the elementals of the upper regions, the air and fire spirits (Sylphs and Salamanders). Their clearest letter or statement about themselves is in the movements of upper parts of plants, the birds, and all the things of air. Direct your attention to bird and insect flight (particularly that of butterflies), plant and leaf movement. Movement is the best starting place. The movement has a rhythmic, shimmering quality. It is alluring and stills the mind. Look for movement everywhere in the garden, alternately holding your awareness on little details, and then spreading it out to perceive the garden movements as a whole.

Now, with a clear knowledge of what you are doing, sit and look around you, giving your imagination as much freedom as it wants. Set your poetic and pictorial fantasy loose, and let it play with what you see. Watch steadily from your sense of 'I'. Hold any impressions that reach you. Don't expect to be sure that you are not deluding yourself, until some time has passed. True spirit impressions formed in high places such as beautiful gardens will always stay. Your own mental creations will quickly fade. The way to check for what is a true picture of the spirits that show themselves in this way is simply to repeat the procedure and see what stays. In essence it is exactly like learning to read. Once you have learned the letters you can piece together words and eventually sentences. From this under-standing of the sentence, a picture can be created in your mind's eye.

Watch the language of form and movement in the leaves, flowers, birds, and clouds, and you will get a clear impression of what the spirits concerned with them look like. This impression will be a kind of psychic vision, including distinct colour impressions just like external vision but it will be very much more deeply connected with feelings of knowing and sensations in your heart.

When you have gained some impression of the beings expressing themselves in the individual events scattered around your garden, try to grasp something of a clear-cut being surrounding one particular tree, or bush. Look for impressions there. They are more a combination of spirit forces. More a word than an individual letter in the spirit language of the garden. Form and movement will combine to tell of a spirit born out of this mixture, and who is deeply concerned with this one bush. A sense of individuality is present in these combined spirits, and when the bush is happy the spirit feels fulfilment. The feeling it has can best be described as being like the feeling when the last notes of a favourite melody finally resolve, the whole tune becomes obviously complete. These plant spirits live permanently in this kind of feeling in a harmonious garden. They radiate this feeling as you will find when you perceive them.

Such beings as these are also discernible in the atmosphere, perhaps at a distance from your garden. They hover in the air around one central dominant form that reaches down into the ground, growing out of it as it were. This is the spirit of the garden, or more probably the whole area in which your garden lies. These spirits are the hardest to gain visual impressions of, but they are there. Such spirits as these are also present over entire towns. They take very different shapes according to the activity of the town they are concerned with. A university town spirit looks or, more commonly, feels different from a spirit of a country village, or an industrial town. Such spirits of the latter are to some extent non-existent. As spirits become more evolved, and mingle with whole entities rather than simple elements, they consequently become harder to perceive for the simple reason that they require some sort of action to become apparent. Looking on is not enough. To know these more advanced spirits takes a committed act from the individual who wants to know more about them. Healing Angels will only show when medicine is practised with high intent. The so-called Muses, spirits of art and human form-creating, will only become apparent when a work of art is produced. This property places such spirits largely beyond the realms of psychic perception alone, and more into the domain of personal life and personal vocation. To know the language of the higher spirits your actions are all-important.

So let me leave you with the following simple method of perceiving the personal spirit of your home . . . Your House Angel. Participation in this ritual will bring a great increase pf psychic perception.

In one corner of your main room place a bowl of salt; this is the earth element. In the next place a bowl of water. In the next place some incense — this is the air corner — incense sticks are easily available. And in the fourth corner place a lighted candle. Stand in the middle and speak out loud, one or two clear sentences, addressed to the Angel personally. Request in the name of all that is good, that it might bestow as much love, wisdom and harmony on your dwelling and its occupants as it can.

Disconnect yourself from psychic thoughts with a deliberate effort of will, and casually go and have a cup of tea or something. As the days go by, you will be pleasantly surprised!

INDEX

abdomen
  popular view of 86
  psychic energy of 104
Air
  as element 30−1
  Sylphs as elementals of 172,
    181, 184
ancient ideas
  and elements 25−9
  psychic awareness in 24−5
  and spirits 171−2
angels 171−2
  healing 186
  house 186−7
  and mankind 183
animal, mineral, vegetable
    (exercise) 78−9
apparitions see ghosts;
    hallucinations; visions
Archangels (spiritual beings)
    171
art, spirits of (Muses) 186
astrology, symbols in 50
Asuras (dark spiritual beings)
    172
atmosphere
  deliberate creation of
    for clairaudience 174
    for crystal ball reading
      150
  detecting spirits in 186
  and elementals 181
  and ghosts 179−81
attitude, importance of
  correct vii−viii, 9−10,
    63−8, 132−3, 135
auras
  around head, (clairvoyance
    exercise II) 93−5
  and direct clairvoyance
    162−5
  human body, colours of
    104, 162−3
awareness
  bodiless 168
    see also death; spirits(s)
  psychic, how to use 69−82
  of self, in direct
    clairvoyance 158−9
    'knock-knock' exercise
      158−9
  spiritual 169−87
awe and reverence 65−7, 69

basic rhythms (exercise) 102
Beelzebub 172
birds, detecting Sylphs and
    Salamanders in movement
    of 184
blood, movement of 99
bodiless awareness 168

see also death; spirit(s)
body see human body
brain
  popular view of 86
  psychic view as
    filter/resistor 89
  spine as 99
  see also head
breath
  movement of 99
  and pulse beat 100
breathing technique for
    trance 153

candle
  in House Angel ritual 187
  power (exercise) 58−9
    and clairvoyant
      perception of human
      body 93
  in scrying 152
chaos, spirits of 172
Cherubim (spiritual beings)
    172
childhood, veneration felt in
    65−7
children, psychic awareness
    in 23−4
Christian Church, spirits
    named by 171−2
clairaudience (spirit voices)
    158, 173−6
  seashell method to cultivate
    173−4, 176
clairvoyance (psychic seeing)
  exercises
    (I) other faces appearing
      91−2
    (II) seeing auras 93−5
  growth in, exercises and 16
  imagination and 41−4
  purpose or point of 40
collective spirits 186
colour, ability to see psychic
    cues (exercise) 76
  of plants 81−2
  techniques 77
  of voice 161, 164−5
communication with
    departed ones 178−9
  see also spiritualism
concentration 69−71, 74
  in clairaudience 174−5
  shifting, in seeing auras 164
confidence, need for
  in direct clairvoyance 158
  in fortune telling 139−40
conflict and irresolution in
    dreams 126−7
confusion, caused by
    elemental penetration 181

consciousness
  altered state after death
    176−9
  and unconsciousness 119
contact with individual
    spirits after death 172
  and spiritualism 173
cross, rotating (exercise)
crystal ball reading 149−66
  alternative speculums
    151−2
  psychic sneezing 154−6
  scrying 149−50
    as exercise 152−4
crystal(s)
  observing (mineral, animal,
    vegetable exercise) 78−9
  in psychometry 148

dark, humans as creatures of
    110−11
day, mood of different times
    of 114−15
death
  and ghosts 179−80
    types of 180−1
  and higher spirits 181−7
  and life 176−9
  and spirit 167−87
    and clairaudience
      173−5
    departure of 177−9
  and spiritualism 173
  what is it? 176−7
departure of the spirit 177−9
detachment, when fortune
    telling 141
Devil
  Tarot card 48
diaphragm 100−2
direct clairvoyance (being
    psychic) 156−66
  and aura 162−4
  and symbol 164−6
  ways of interpreting 157−8
Dominions (spiritual beings)
    172
dreams/dreaming 108−31
  conflict and irresolution in
    126−7
  and human body 125−6
  land of 123−4
  major questions 124−5
  meaning of 121−31
  praying for 121
  psychic approach to
    121−31
  questions within 127−9
  recalling 122−3, 129−31
  revisiting (exercise) 130−1
  state and clairaudience 175

About the Author:

Carl Rider is a writer and clairvoyant who specialises in psychic and paranormal research. He is the co-author of *The Psychic Explorer*, with Jonathan Cainer. He lives in Yorkshire and Wales.